harry whittington
web of murder

After selling his first short story to United Features
for $15 in 1943, Harry Whittington went on to write
crime, suspense, western, and romance novels under
his own name and such pseudonyms as Whit Harrison,
Hallam Whitney, Harry White, Kell Holland, Clay
Stuart, Harriet Kathryn Myers, and Ashley Carter.
He died in 1990.

web
of murder

harry whittington

VINTAGE CRIME / **BLACK LIZARD**

vintage books • a division of random house, inc. • new york

First Vintage Crime/Black Lizard Edition, May 1993

Copyright © 1958 by Harry Whittington
Copyright renewed 1986 by Harry Whittington

Library of Congress Cataloging-in-Publication Data
Whittington, Harry, 1915–
Web of murder/by Harry Whittington. — 1st Vintage Crime/Black Lizard ed.
p.   cm. — (Vintage Crime/Black Lizard)
ISBN 0-679-74068-6
I. Title.   II. Series.
PS3545.H896 W43   1993
813'.54—dc20   92-50691   CIP

Manufactured in the United States of America
10 9 8 7 6 5 4 3 2 1

web
of murder

1

I kept asking questions but they couldn't remember any other details. The three of them sat in my office, glancing at each other. My secretary came in and I had them run through the story again, but Laura's taking notes unnerved them and they were already changing what they'd told me.

I leaned back and studied them. The old woman appeared to be about sixty-five. Her sister was a mousy thirty-year-old who twisted her fingers and patted Mrs. Homelin's hand, but otherwise added nothing. Mouse's husband, sprawled in a leather chair, was the real doll. He was the boy with all the answers—and the only one of the three who hadn't witnessed the tragedy.

Suddenly I'd had enough for one night, and called a halt. I told them to return the following evening at seven and in the meantime to sort out the angles so we could get together a coherent brief. I reminded them that murder was serious and they'd never keep Mrs. Homelin's son out of the electric chair by contradicting each other.

Laura showed them out. I glanced at my wrist watch, feeling depleted in a way that had nothing to do with the time.

I stared at Laura, thinking about what I had to do, knowing the answer was simple. I had to fire her.

"What?" I said. She was standing rigidly, her face flushed, and she had said something.

"It's late. After ten. Is that all, Mr. Brower?"

Her gray suit had faint blue threads in it. Her white shirt was buttoned at the base of her throat. I remembered I'd hired her because at first glance I'd decided she was just another strawberry blonde who'd never disrupt my office. That was six months ago. After she'd been with me a while I began to see things in her, and I began to see she was different, and not like any other woman at all.

First thing that got inside me was when I saw she wasn't just what she was pretending to be. Nine to five she was cool, sedate and efficient. I got to wondering what she did away from the office. Where'd she go for amusement? What music did she enjoy? Did she drink? Dance? And sometimes her hazel eyes had flecks in them, fear or old hurts, secretive and hidden.

I shrugged it off. So Laura wasn't the simple, uncomplex soul she appeared. It was not my affair. She knew what I wanted in a secretary and played the part expertly.

"Sure. That's all," I said. "Thanks, Laura."

"They're odd, aren't they?" She frowned. "You can't tell what to believe."

I shrugged. Her hair twisted into red-gold ringlets at the nape of her neck. "You haven't been in this racket very long. You'll believe what they want you to believe. You'll keep going over it with them until they believe it themselves. Finally you'll take it to a court and try to make a jury believe it."

"They seemed so nervous. Especially the man."

I smiled wryly. "A dangerous character. A no-good who wants to feel important. I'll get a deposition from him and then send him out of town. I couldn't afford to have him on my side."

"You—really think you can save her son from the electric chair?"

"If I didn't, I wouldn't have taken the case."

I watched her walk toward the door. She paused, hand on the knob. That silhouette could keep you awake nights.

"I know you're tired, Mr. Brower—"

"No. What's wrong?"

She hesitated. "I want to ask a favor—and I hate to—"

"Why should you? Six months, and you haven't asked a favor. You've caught me in an expansive mood. What's troubling you?" I nodded toward a chair.

She sat down and crossed her knees, gripping shorthand pad and pencils tightly in her lap. "It's—this girl friend of mine, Mr. Brower. Her husband—well, he got into trouble, stealing from his firm—and was sent to prison for three years. He's served a third of his term and is eligible for parole, but needs help—from a good attorney."

"Have your friend come in and see me."

She chewed her lip. "She—might not have much money."

"That's all right, Laura. For a friend of yours we can work out something."

She stirred in her chair. "No. I mean—if it's all right with you—she's had so much trouble and expense and all—I'd rather keep this—about the money—between you and me."

I should have frowned. Inside I was frowning; money or lack of it should be on the table between lawyer and clients. "We can work that out, too."

She went on sitting there for some moments, as though she wanted to say more. It grew silent in the office, silent in the quiet building. It was as if everything paused in that moment, waiting for something.

Summit was an overgrown town, but no city, and in Summit I was well known. I drove home slowly, telling myself to get her out of my mind. The further Cora and I drifted apart, the more I thought about Laura. First I told myself I was too smart to go for that love malarkey. I wanted her. It was that simple. I could have her for a weekend somewhere, if I could arrange it, and never think of her again. Or I could be really smart and fire her.

But I didn't fire her. I didn't like to think about that office without her in it. I didn't suggest a weekend somewhere, either. At home I was wound tighter and tighter. Cora started talking about how I was working too hard, having too much on my mind, and how I needed to see a doctor or a headshrinker. Finally she had made an appointment with Dr. Murray, but I laughed at that. I didn't need a doctor to tell me what was the matter with me. I didn't believe any doctor could explain why I couldn't get Laura out of my mind even when I wanted to. But just the same I couldn't do it. The weeks went by and it got worse, much worse.

I turned off Forest Drive into my place without really knowing how I got there.

This house had cost Cora forty-five thousand. Since it was a single-storied, three-bedroom ranch-type, the twenty-odd thousands had gone into extras—landscaping, tile, interior decorating and the swimming pool that stayed empty and leaf-pocked all winter. Sitting back from Forest

Drive in an acre of sodded grass, manicured elms and chest-high hedge, it wasn't nearly the most expensive house along here, but it was the smartest, and even Cora's cattiest enemy grudgingly admitted this. Inside, it was the sort of place where if you tossed an opened newspaper on a coffee table, the entire layout was unbalanced.

But it wouldn't matter. Cora wouldn't leave it there long.

I parked in the carport and went through the sun-parlor entrance, carrying my briefcase. Cora was doing her intricate needlework in the front room.

I started toward the kitchen.

"Charley?"

"Yes, Cora."

"Where have you been?"

I dropped my briefcase in the foyer and leaned on the door jamb. "Where have I been? Haven't some of your well-intentioned friends reported to you yet?"

"Don't be smart, Charley. It's after eleven. I just asked. Shouldn't I be interested in you? What else do I have to be interested in?"

"God knows. I don't have the secret information service you do."

"You're in a foul mood. Why, Charley? I'm the one who should be. I had dinner alone, went to the Myers' and played bridge, and what could I tell them?"

"I don't know, Cora. What could you tell them?"

"That I never see you. That I live my solitary existence, and you have your life, your work, your friends, all the things you'd rather do than come home."

"I had to work late."

"I don't believe you."

"I don't care."

"Of course you don't care. Why should Charles R. Brower care what his wife thinks. I called your office. I got no answer."

"Why, I was out at the Brahma. As you know, I'm irresistible. Two women were waiting in my car when I left my office—"

"What time did you leave it?"

"Lord, Cora. If I were rich as you, I wouldn't work late. I'd come home and watch you do needlework."

"Is there something you'd rather I did? Maybe you'd like it better if I ran around. I could, you know. Plenty of men are interested in me. Would you like it if I was drinking out at the Brahma?"

"Why not? We might run into each other."

"That would be sweet, wouldn't it? Maybe you don't care what people think about you, but I do."

"Cora, I was just going to have a drink. Will you have one with me?"

"You always think I'm so happy because Father left me money. Father wanted me to have the things I wanted. What do I have? A husband too busy for me, too wrapped up in himself—"

"You want a Martini, a Collins?"

"I hate whisky, and you know it."

"A Martini is made with gin."

"To me it's all the same. It makes me ill."

"You mind if I have one?"

"I want to have interests, too, Charley. But you're not interested. You want that office. I could give you anything."

Sure. Anything except money. Her old man had willed her half a million he'd accumulated like a squirrel. Sinful to spend, sinful to waste, sinful to throw it away on pleasure, hoard it, stack it up. And Cora inherited all his traits along with his money.

"I want money of my own. Unfortunately, I know no way to get it except by working."

"I wouldn't mind your working, but I hate the way you run around with women—"

"You like it better if I ran around with men?"

"Don't be silly. You know what I mean. My friends see you. I know what's going on, all right."

I walked past her, opened the portable bar, and mixed a Martini five to one. There was no ice. I carried the mixing pitcher into the kitchen.

I returned with the ice-frosted glass and sat down beside Cora. She was heavy, steadily getting heavier. We were in our middle thirties. I was showing my age, but with Cora I had to look at it. Her blonde hair was smoothly set, but looking at her, all I could think of was a Swedish kitchen girl. Cora wasn't Swedish, and was as lost in the kitchen as she was in the bedroom. You've got yourself a wonderful existence, Charley Brower. Wonderful. Everything a man could want. My trouble was I coveted nice things; my tastes ran to Cadillacs, caviar and cashmere jackets. My income was rising, but an average income for an attorney runs around ten thousand a year and I was just hitting that. In this profession it takes time—time I hated wasting when Cora was loaded with the stuff and didn't even understand how to enjoy it.

I put my arm around her.

"Do I give you a bad time, Cora?"

"You don't make it easy."

"Come taste my drink."

"I don't want to taste your drink. I don't have to get drunk to enjoy myself."

I pulled her closer. She leaned toward me awkwardly.

"Let's go to bed, Cora."

She didn't even know what I was talking about.

"Not yet, Charley. I want to finish this line. If I stop, these stitches won't be right."

"Hire it done."

"It's not the same thing at all, Charley."

I sighed, finished off my drink, got up, and poured another.

"Charley, you're not going to get so drunk you can't make it to bed, are you?"

"What difference does it make?" I spoke across my shoulder. "I won't disturb you in your bedroom."

"Charley, don't start that again. You aren't going to start that again, are you?"

"God forbid." I finished off the second Martini, looking at Cora. Swedish kitchen girl. All that money. Five hundred grand. All mine when she died. If she died. Cora was strong as a cow; she was going to live forever, hoarding every dime. Forever denying me anything she disapproved—and she'd been reared to disapprove anything related to frivolous pleasure and vanity. The way she doled out money to me was insulting, and when she gave me fifty dollars to throw away she beamed as if she were Lady Bountiful.

When I started from the room she wanted to know where

I was going. I remembered to be polite. I'd cost her a lot of money getting where I was. And where was I? I fell across my bed, thinking here was the end of another gracious evening at home with the Charles R. Browers. I wondered if Cora ever guessed how much I wanted her to die.

I awoke the next morning in the same sour mood, and the man awaiting me in my office did nothing to brighten my day.

Frank Vanness.

A cop.

You've said that, you've said about all there is to say about him. You can describe him, tell him where he lives and what he eats and what he wears, but when you've said *cop* you've said it all. It was his whole life. He told me how it was being a cop, and I believed him. Let any man step out of line, he's got the belt coming to him and ought to expect it. Frank Vanness was the man to apply the belt.

"A man pulls something, I owe him no consideration. Nothing. He steps out on his wife and gets in trouble. Why should I keep his wife from knowing? He asked for it. Once a man breaks a law, he can expect consequences. Not just some of them. All of them."

Great company for me, the way I felt that morning.

When I felt better, I kidded Vanness, told him he'd wreck ninety-nine per cent of marriages, overflow the jails if he practiced such ideas. He had no sense of humor about it. "We got laws, That's what we got 'em for, to obey. Right?"

I had gotten involved in his investigations on a couple of divorce cases where the wife had called in the police, or they'd been summoned on a peace-breach. I asked him if it wasn't possible that a married woman might truly love some man other than her husband. He gave me a look of contempt. "A no-good?" he said. "Put this in your book, Counsellor. If she'll step out on her husband *with* you, she'll step out *on* you later. They ain't no exceptions."

I'd long since stopped arguing with him. Sometimes I

wondered how he'd existed forty years in this complex society with such unrealistic views, but I never inquired. Like most lawyers, I disliked cops, and I especially disliked Frank Vanness. When he opposed you on a witness stand, he was a stubborn nut to crack, a man who gave a jury the impression of being right, even when he was wrong.

"In this report on the Homelin case, Frank," I said, "it shows you investigated the death?"

"That's right."

"Did you think it looked like self-defense?"

"Hah!"

"Justifiable homicide?"

"Never heard of it . . . Oh, sure, I've heard the words from guys like you that make a living off words. But I never saw it. Murder is a cold killing, and it's a crime. I never heard of a case where taking another life was justifiable."

"They say the old man beat the old woman, was cruel to all of them, and had repeatedly threatened the boy."

"If the boy didn't like things, he could clear out."

"What about the old lady?"

"If she didn't like her life with the old man let her get out. Nobody said she was his slave."

I stared at him. "Maybe there were reasons they had to stay on that farm. The old man had the money. The wife was getting old. Farming was all the Homelin kid knew."

"All right. So they had a good thing with the old man. Let them expect it wasn't going to be like heaven on earth. They knew the old man had a violent temper, liked to rule his house the way his father had ruled it before him—"

"That can get pretty sickening, Frank."

"Enough to excuse a murder? Listen, that Homelin kid lay in his bed night after night and planned how he was going to kill that old man. Sure, I know you been talking to the son-in-law. He wants that farm. He's got the old woman and the girl all worked up. They think they can get that other boy out of jail and he'll work on that farm for them because they know he's guilty of murder."

"You expect to testify for the prosecution, Frank?"

"If they ask me."

"I got both the cops that arrived on the scene."

He shrugged. "What do they know? You want to know

why they're beat cops? Because they know just enough about police work to blow a whistle."

"Couldn't you ever be wrong, Frank?"

"About murder? No. I seen too many of them. I seen all kinds. They all add up to one thing: murder. Murderers have got a smell, and I can smell them out. You know my record? One case not solved—and I can put my hand on the guy who did that, but he's got an influential family and I couldn't get anything but circumstantial evidence against him—evidence that had to be true. I had to turn him loose. That hurts. It muddies up my record. It won't happen again."

"I've a good case, Frank. You'll look bad."

"It won't be the first time. But I'm right. The kid jumped the old man with murderous intent, and I can prove it. Killers are stupid, all of them. I never saw a case yet I couldn't break."

"I'm going to beat you this time, Frank."

He shrugged. "You won't. No lawyer will, Counsellor. If a cop does his work right, no lawyer can change it."

"That's where you're wrong. There are always angles."

"My friend said she would let me know," Laura said when Vanness was gone. She stood beside my desk, tucked into a tailored tan frock with deep-cut neck. "She's so shy. She—she's afraid of you, Mr. Brower. It'll take time. She'll have to get up her nerve."

"She'll get it up if she wants anything done for her husband."

"Oh, yes. She will. It's just that she's felt so unhappy—afraid of what people will think of her—because of what her husband did and all. But she wants help. She'll let me know."

I nodded, trying to concentrate on the briefs on my desk. She went on standing there. After a moment I looked up. Maybe it was the reflection of the sun through the window. Her face looked pink-tinted.

"I want to thank you. It's fine, what you're doing. I know you're doing it for me."

"What's a friend for. Laura?"

I heard her heavy inhalation. "I wouldn't know, Mr. Brower. I haven't had very many."

"Now you're kidding me. A pretty girl like you—"

"I'm not pretty—"

"No. All right, you're hideous. No wonder you have no friends. Going around doing things for them—like what you're doing for this friend what's-her-name and her husband?"

"Mary? Oh, well, she's different. We both went to business college at the same time. Everything troubled her and she had to tell me about it. I took her in to live with me—until she got married. I was glad to have her. I never had anybody, you know."

"No. I didn't."

"Well, my parents died when I was twelve. I lived for a few years with relatives, but they had no room for me, really. I was a burden. I hate to be a burden on any one. I always like to pay my own way, whatever I do. Guess it's because I was a burden for so long."

I stood up, walked to her. I touched her shoulder. I could feel the heat of her against my palm.

I kept my voice level. "You worried about my fee, Laura? Is that it?"

"Partly. I know you'll let me pay you any way I can. But I want you to let me pay you."

There was no sense pretending I didn't know what she meant. It was in the way her hazel eyes brushed mine and fell away. She did not move away from the desk, or away from me, but stood waiting.

I looked down at her, feeling the way my pulse pounded, the way I wanted her.

I'd have to fire her. We'd turn this place into a love nest in less time than it would take to tell it. Mornings not opening the front door, evenings working late. Three hours for lunch. I needed something, but not the mess that that would be.

I was going to get her out of there, and get my mind back to work. All right, I didn't have a heaven out on Forest Drive, but I had my career, I knew what I wanted. This was sticking my hand into a furnace, reaching for something I really didn't even want.

All I had to do was tell her I was going to have to get another girl. Her work was satisfactory, but . . . It didn't matter what I told her, anything would do. I had to get her out.

I didn't believe it even when I felt my hand moving on the small of her back, felt the way she quivered against my hand, the way her body moved close against my body. I pulled her face up against mine and saw her eyes close like a tired baby's, and her lips parted as if she were hungry and thirsty and needing—all the things I was. I was shaking all over. But for a moment I thought I was wrong about everything. Her parted mouth was cool against my lips. She held her body rigid.

Her eyes opened and our gazes met. For an instant it was as if we hated each other. And then she cried out and her lips came hard against mine.

For a long time I knew only one thing: I wasn't going to fire her.

"I shouldn't have let you. What will you think of me?"

"I think you're exciting."

"Yes. But what else? What do you think I am? Kissing you like that in the office. What if somebody had walked in?"

I didn't have my breath back yet.

"You must think I'm terrible," she said. "Do you want me to quit?"

"What for?" Five minutes ago I was going to fire her. Now I was ready to beg her to stay. "Why do you want to quit?"

"We can't do this. I don't know what we were thinking."

"I know what I was thinking. What were you thinking?"

"I'd spoil everything for you, I'd be bad for you."

"I'm a big boy. Stop worrying about me. I can take care of myself."

"But maybe you can't. I had no right—"

"Is there somebody else, Laura?"

"What?"

"Another guy? Somebody you love? I know so little about you."

"And I about you." She shook her head. "There's nobody else—like that, I mean. Nobody else at all. Fellows I dance with, go to the movies with. Nothing—like this."

"Do they thrill you, Laura? When they hold you?"

She pulled away, walked to the window. "Well, you can laugh if you want. But—I never knew I could feel this way."

"What are you talking about?"

"I never knew a man could make a girl feel the way—the way you make me feel. I knew men got excited. I just never knew a girl was supposed to."

I caught her in my arms. "Good Lord you are young."

She held herself rigidly. "No. That has nothing to do with it."

"What has?"

"I just never felt this way about anybody else."

"Thank God."

"No. It's terrible."

"Why?"

"You don't have to ask that. I work here. You're my boss—unless you want to fire me. I wouldn't blame you."

"You'll have to quit if you want to get away from me."

"I—better get back out to my desk. I have a lot of work."

"Forget it."

"No. I've got to keep busy."

"All right."

"Don't be angry, Mr.—Charley . . ." She smiled.

"Now what are you laughing at?"

"If you knew how I've thought about that—just saying your name—just calling you Charley."

"It sounds fine."

"Oh, no. I've got to stop it. I'll have to resign."

"You're sore at me?"

"You know better. It's just what happened—"

"You wanted it to happen, didn't you?"

"Yes. I guess so. I've thought about it a lot. I guess we both wanted it. But that doesn't matter. It can't happen any more . . . not if I'm to stay here."

"All right. If that's what you want."

"Oh, Charley. You know that isn't what I want. But that's the way it has to be."

"All right."

I got rid of Mrs. Homelin and her in-laws in less than an hour that night.

Laura said, "Well, good night."

"Good night, who?"

"Good night, Charley."

"How do you get home?" I had never asked before, never even wondered.

"Bus. Takes about half an hour."

"Seems a long time."

"I'm used to it."

"Why not let me drive you home?"

"It's out of the way. I couldn't let you."

We ate supper at the Crystal Inn. It was a hundred miles out Highway 41. It was a little before ten when we got there. I didn't even know where the miles went. I got to talking about Cora, and in the warm car, with the hum of the motor and the faint dashlight across us, nothing else was real. It was as if we were hurtling through space in a vacuum and nothing outside our racing sphere could ever touch us.

It was odd, too, the terrible need we felt, and yet we sat in that car with only our hands touching. It was enough for the moment, all the excitement in us met and fused in our fingers.

I didn't try to pretend I was a misunderstood husband, or anything like that. I told Laura the truth. It was just that Cora and I were meant for each other like snow and Havana. I had met Cora during my second year in college, and whether I really wanted it or not, her father under-wrote the rest of my law school. Cora wanted me, and old man wanted Cora to have the best. He said my law school-ing was the best investment he could ever make for Cora. When her father died, Cora and I got married. It was too late for anything else.

"Couldn't you get a divorce?"

"I've asked her. Don't worry, I've asked her. It's seemed obvious even to Cora that she hasn't been thrilled by me since six months before we got married—"

"What does she want if she doesn't want you?"

"I don't know. Her home. Her bridge. Her needlework. Me there, when she wants me."

"Sounds terrible."

"Oh, no. It's fine. It's like hitting yourself in the head with a hammer."

"Couldn't you just go away?"

"Looks like it, doesn't it? I mean, Cora has her own money. It isn't as if she depended on me. Matter of fact, I've been dependent on her. It isn't as though we have any children—anything to keep us together."

"Don't you owe yourself anything?"

"I don't know. What am I? A lawyer. Like every lawyer I've got those ambitions. State senate. Judgeship. Washington. Hell, I don't know. But I'm a lawyer. Sometimes I think I'm a lawyer because I need to be. I've been one for ten years now. It's all I know. I could throw it all away, and what would I have? I wouldn't even have anything to live on."

"Don't you have a bank account? I'm not trying to pry."

"I know you're not."

"I'm just interested. Terribly interested."

"Sure. We have a joint account. Cora might let me go away with another woman, but not with her money. She'd hound me off the edge of the earth.

"Poor Charley."

"Don't feel sorry for me. I got what I asked for."

"Oh, you didn't. You couldn't possibly have known."

"No. But now I know."

"You could be happy. You could be so happy."

Our hands tightened on the seat between us.

"Yes," I said. "I could be happy."

"You've got to do something."

I nodded. That was when I knew for certain. She was right. I had to do something.

The car raced through the darkness. The sound it made was the only sound on the highway.

L aura didn't mention her troubled friend. In the next few days I forgot all about her.

I prowled like a caged panther in the circle between my

home and my office. I knew what I was thinking about, but I kept pushing it out of my mind and would not let myself think about it.

When I was with Laura, I was all right. When I wasn't with her, I was obsessed. All I could do was wonder where she was and what she was doing.

I'd get to my office early and wait for her.

Most days I liked my office. Like everything else Cora and I had together, it had cost a lot of money—the correct leather chairs, the low desk and the judge's chair behind it. Everything had a clean, uncluttered look. I'd spent Cora's money extravagantly for the neutral-gray rug, the pad beneath it. It squashed pleasantly under a client's shoes. It gave them a feeling of confidence in me. And there was more. They quit thinking in terms of peanuts in fees by the time they'd crossed from door to chair. My law library was the best in Summit. The County Bar Association had assessed all its members a few years ago and equipped a central law library. It was no better than mine—and its shelves were not half so good.

All right. I was proud of what I possessed. I wanted to keep it, improve it. Most days I could close off my mind, consciously block the tensions without the tranquilizers Cora took twice a day, and three times when under stress. I could force myself to forget the things that drove me, the basic needs and hungers that come to a man. Sure, I was being robbed, but every man compromised, didn't he? Nobody got everything he wanted. I had Cora and her money. I had my law practice, my law library, my reputation in the bar fraternity—among lawyers I was respected and feared, nobody used gimmicks or tried to pull chairs out from under Charley Brower.

I stood looking down at Main Street. Four hundred thousand people in a town planned for sixty thousand. I had what I wanted here in Summit, didn't I?

And then I could smell Laura even before I could hear her on the expensive carpeting.

"I missed you," Laura said.

"I've been waiting for you."

"I don't live when I'm away from you. I have no life away from this office."

I pulled her close against me. "We can't go on like this, Laura."

"No."

"I can't stand it."

"I hate it too, Charley. What are we going to do?"

"I know what I want. I want you. I'd like to take a honeymoon with you—maybe a year in the Bahamas—"

"Only a year? That's not much of a honeymoon."

"Only a year in the Bahamas."

She laughed. "Oh, Charley. What am I going to do? Why don't I quit? Why don't I go away?"

"You want me to lose my mind?"

"What else is there, Charley?"

"Don't give up. She can't live forever."

"Isn't it terrible, Charley? But that's what I think—I lie awake at night thinking it. If only she'd die."

"She never will."

"Too bad she isn't dead." She shivered. "Do you hate me for saying that, Charley?"

"Why should I hate you? It's what I think. It's what we both think."

"Yes. I know. It scares me—just knowing it."

It was between us all the time. When we looked at each other, we saw it in each other's eyes. When we spoke, it was behind the most commonplace things we said.

"You've got to stop me thinking like this, Charley."

"No. It's better now that we've brought it out in the open. What's she got to live for? A bank full of money that she chews like a cow on its cud."

A tremor went through her and she gripped my arms, staring into my eyes. "But—we'll never do it, will we, Charley?"

"I don't know."

"Killing somebody . . . How terrible that is . . . You don't know."

I walked away from her and stood at the window. People crawling around down there, walking over each other, snarling. Why didn't they kill? Because they were afraid. No other reason.

"You're wrong," I said. "I know how terrible it is to kill. But I know something else—how impossible it is getting away with it."

"We're not going to do it, Charley. We're insane even to think about it."

I turned around. "You're wrong. We *are* going to do it."

"We?" She leaned against the desk.

"We. Us. You and I. All we're doing now is trying to figure how we can do it and get away with it. You know it."

"We couldn't, Charley." Her teeth chattered. But the look in her eyes was anxiety and compulsion all fused. I pulled my gaze away from her.

"Yes. We could."

"How? How could we take her life? What's she ever done to us?"

"She's kept us apart. She's got the money we need. And that's what stops us—the money. Isn't it, Laura?"

"If you say so, Charley."

"Sure. She's no good even to herself. She'd be better off dead. We want her money . . . and we want to get away with it."

She stood silently against the desk for a long time. At last she whispered, "An accident, Charley? Accidental death?"

I laughed, a sharp, harsh sound I didn't recognize.

"You mean because I'm a lawyer? I could beat the accidental death rap? Oh, no. That's too risky. Be glad I'm a lawyer. I can tell you. Accidents just never are accidents. Somebody is to blame for every accident that happens—and when there's money involved somebody will keep picking at that accident. No. The first thing we don't want is to get mixed up with an insurance company or a jury.

"But you believe you can help the Homelin woman and her son."

"That's different. The risk is theirs. I'm her agent—her representative and her counsel. Anything I do for her is privileged—another gimmick lawyers have contrived in courts to be sure justice is the only accident." I turned around. "But when I am personally involved in an accident, or a trial, everything changes. Accidents, or anything that might involve insurance, is out."

"Is she heavily insured?"

"No. Not heavily—not for a woman with half a million. There's a great deal more insurance on me." Again that burst of strange laughter crossed my mouth. "You might profit more by killing me."

At first her face went white, as if I had struck her. Then she said, her smile uncertain. "I will, darling. I will. But not that way. Slowly. I'm going to love you to death."

"I can't wait to start dying."

The next morning I was waiting for her when she entered the outer office. I called her. She still had her hat on when she came through the door.

I said, "You want to go through with it?"

She paused, frowning. She bit at her underlip. "I want you, Charley. You know that."

"Then you want to go through with it?"

"All right."

"Say it."

She drew a deep breath. "I want to go through with it, Charley. With you."

"Come here."

When she stood beside me, her shoulder against my arm, I started talking, fast, because I wanted to get it all out; make her understand how clever we were going to be.

"Murder is something that's got to be carefully figured out. You can't say that some people get away with murder, and take a chance on the law of averages. Averages have nothing to do with it. You can't afford a loss when you mess with murder, and you can't afford a bad guess. You know who gets away with murder?"

She was staring at me, as if carried along on the tension of my voice. "Who, Charley?"

"Professional killers. Because they leave both ends of an alley open. But we're not professionals. We can't hire it done, it's something we've got to do ourselves. But murder is the biggest crime. We can't hope just to commit a murder and get away with it. Murder is too big, too glaring, has too many people picking at it."

"All right, Charley. I trust your judgment. If you want to back out, let's forget it."

"I didn't say that. All I said is we've got to be smart. There can be no chance of getting involved in a trial—none of those clever legal angles that *might* get you free. I've been practicing for ten years in circuit courts. I know what juries are. Juries are prejudices, ignorances, what a man ate for breakfast, how he gets along with his wife, what he's got on his mind. A jury will take a liking to a lawyer or a defendant, and nothing else is important. I'm not risking my neck to the judgment of twelve stupid people two lawyers have allowed to sit in a jury box. We've got to stay out of court. We've got to fix it so we not only are never caught, but are never even suspected."

"Yes, Charley." She closed her hands on my arms. "I know you can do that . . . I've known it all along."

"It won't be easy. It will take time, and it can't be hurried. If we do it at all, we've got to go slowly, pave the way for the murder."

"Oh, Charley. If we could only run—get away."

"Sure. Act big. Take a big chance. You win big—but you lose big. That's just fine, but I want to keep what I have. I want to stay here, Laura. First of all I want you, but I want that money too, and all it'll buy—all I've missed. I can't have it by risking everything and running. I want to get away with it. I don't even want to be suspected."

"But is there a way?"

"Sure. I told you. A little at a time. And the good thing about it is you don't have to keep looking over your shoulder."

"I don't understand."

"Do you have to?"

"All right—I trust you."

"And you're with me? All the way? Say it."

"I'm in it, Charley. All the way. With you."

Her eyes were bright—green and bright.

I left the office at noon. I had to get out of there, away from Laura, where I could think clearly. Near her, there was the scent of her, the need to touch her.

I walked down the corridor. A man spoke to me twice before I even realized there was anybody else going toward the elevator.

"Oh, hi, Doc."

He laughed. "Boy, where was your mind?" Ed Murray had his suite of offices on the same floor with mine. He was carrying his medical kit, hurrying to a call. "You had an appointment with me, Charley. Over a week ago. I told you you need a physical. You've been driving yourself too long, too hard. We can't keep doing that, Charley. It begins to show."

I laughed at him. "Look who's talking," I said. "The walking scarecrow."

"With me, it's different. I'm run down like this because I don't know any good doctors. You've no excuse, Charley—you know me. Why don't you drop in this afternoon?"

"Sure."

I wasn't about to waste my time in any doctor's office. Cora had started this foolishness weeks ago. She'd said I was off my feed, that I snapped at her, that I never smiled any more. She'd called Ed, and he'd agreed with her. But I didn't need a doctor; I knew what was the matter with me.

I'd had it. Up to here. If they thought I was slightly crazy, all right. I was. Maybe you never think about murder until you're pushed to the brink. I'd been pushed. I hadn't stopped working for a minute in the last sixteen years. College and law school had depleted me. I'd stayed in the upper third of my class, but I drudged. Maybe even in the ten years of practice I had begun by looking at things in a slanted, cockeyed way. All the ideals learned in school were quickly beaten out of me, and I fought back with every trick I knew. I saw innocent men convicted and criminals escape justice. I'd begun thinking I represented forces of law and order. I found the courts are places of lawlessness, where intelligent jurors are not wanted, where procedure is so gimmicked that witnesses are restrained from telling important facts and tricked into admitting untruths, half-truths. It had become a racket to me, and the prize went to the smartest racketeer. Now I wanted something else—freedom, and half a million dollars. To get it I had to be smarter than police detectives like Frank Vanness and the FBI cops—men who once had been lawyers and were reputedly clever.

Everything I'd ever believed was burned out of me, and I knew what I wanted. And it was a challenge that I felt was worthy of me. My life staked against Cora's money, my freedom, everything that Laura Meadill was or ever would be.

4

Ididn't go back to the office. At five o'clock I walked into
the house. You could tell Cora was startled to see me.
"Are you sick, Charley?" She put aside her needlework
and swarmed all over me. I thrust down her soft hands.

"I'm all right."

"Dr. Murray called."

"So?"

"You broke an appointment."

"It was nothing definite."

"It's the second one you've broken. He told me."

"All right. So maybe he'll get the idea. I don't want to see
him. I don't need a doctor. I know what's wrong with me."
She exhaled. "What is it, Charley? Me?"

I poured a drink of whisky, straight, warm, and drank it
off. "Why not be honest about it? It's you, partly. Oh, it's
not your fault. You're what you are. And I'm what I am."

"What do you want me to be, Charley? I try. Honestly,
I try."

"Maybe I don't want you to try. Maybe that's it. It's too
late to try. I can't help it. I get cabin fever when I walk into
this place. You suffocate me. I can't help it, Cora." I poured
another drink.

"Please, Charley. You drink too much."

"Would you believe, Cora, I never drink when I'm away
from you? I only need a drink when I'm in this house."

She sank down onto the divan, ran her fingers nervously
over her needlework. "Oh, Charley. Do you need to hurt me?
Is that it, Charley? Do you get pleasure from hurting me?"

I crossed the room and looked down at her. "Cora, I don't
want to hurt you at all."

"But you do."

"Yes. I do. But it's not easy for me, Cora. If you'd give me
a divorce, you'd be out of it."

"No, Charley. You'd be out of it. That's what you mean."

"All right. We'd both be out of it."

"But that's just it, Charley. I don't want to be out of it. If only you'd put all this out of your mind. We could go away somewhere—"

"I don't want to go away."

"You'll get over this, Charley. Goodness knows, this isn't the first time you've asked for a divorce. It won't be the last."

I stared at her. That just goes to show you, Cora, I thought; you don't know me as well as you think you do.

"It is the last time, Cora. I mean it."

"I don't want to talk about it."

"We've got to talk about it, or something terrible's going to happen."

"How can you say that Charley? I'm very pleased with my life. We have a lovely home, lovely friends. I don't know any man so well spoken of as you are. I'm very pleased to be Mrs. Charles Brower."

I wiped the back of my hand across my mouth.

"Besides, Charley. I don't believe in divorce."

"No. I guess you don't." I barked a laugh at her, full of sarcasm. "Do you believe in love, Cora?"

She smiled, shook her head. "Never heard of it. Or—wait a minute, wasn't it something we both caught one spring at college? Very contagious. As I recall, almost everyone contracted it that spring."

"Your recovery was miraculous."

"Now, that's better, Charley. You're smiling."

"Sure. Laugh. What the hell's the use of crying?"

I had tried. I did not want to kill Cora. I wanted to be free, didn't I? Or did I? Or was I just setting it up, making it look good. At that moment I couldn't say. If Cora had agreed to a divorce . . . But she didn't; I had known all along she wasn't going to.

I didn't sleep that night. I felt as though I were on a rack and they were drawing me tighter and tighter.

Laura wanted to have lunch with me the next day. I told her I had to see a client.

"I don't remember any appointment," she said.

I looked up at her. "There wasn't any. I confirmed it last night, by phone."

"I'm sorry, Charley. It's just that—I don't know. You act

so strange. I didn't see you all day yesterday, or last night. You didn't call. Do you want to back out, Charley? You can, if you want to. I'll go away. You can forget all about it."

I came around the desk, fast. I caught her in my arms, pressing my body against hers, feeling all the excitement and warmth that charged from her into me.

"Don't talk like that," I told her. "Don't you ever talk like that again."

Her eyes closed slowly. "All right, Charley. All right."

"Victoria. Victoria Haines."

She turned in the crowded dining room at the Brahma and stared at me for a moment. I smiled to myself, knowing she was too nearsighted to recognize me, too vain to wear glasses.

I moved nearer, and she must have made out the fuzzy lines of me. She smiled and came to me with both hands outstretched.

"Why, Charley, Charley Brower. What are you doing here in the middle of the day? Are you alone?"

"Yes. I was looking for you."

"Oh, you liar. How I love the way you lie. You haven't thought about me in years."

"Don't be silly."

"Have you had lunch?"

"A couple of Martinis. How about joining me, Victoria?"

She chewed at her lip for a quarter of a second. "I'm with a couple of girls—"

"Of course. It's all right."

"Can't you wait just a minute? Let me tell them. I'll be right back." She squeezed my hand. "You don't know how really thrilled I am, Charley."

I watched her walk away, thinking she didn't know how pleased I was, either. I had come here looking for her, and had almost given up when she walked in.

She came back toward the bar, where I leaned on a stool waiting for her. I thought, she's the perfect product of whatever assembly line turns out Victoria Haineses.

Looking at Victoria, you might wonder what she'd be without the beauty salon, the fashion shop, and the shoe stables. But it didn't matter. She was the supremely smooth

result. They bent each brown hair into shape and lacquered
it into place, shaded her eyes and touched up the corners,
suggesting depth to their nearsighted blueness, they high-
lighted the planes of her cheeks, lined her lips. They sup-
ported and accented all her natural endowments. It wasn't
that Victoria Haines was in any sense false. She was well
done. The quality that made her different was her own
inner glow. It seemed to whisper that she would smear the
lipstick, muss the hair, rip off that dress if the stimulation
were there. And better than that, her eyes told you that
you—and only you—could ever accomplish just the correct
stimulation.

We sat down and ordered, and Victoria said again how
excited she was to run into me by such a lovely accident.

I'd helped her get a divorce from Chet Haines. It could
have been messy, but I handled the angles for her, and she
never could forget it. It was as if I had saved her life—that
was the way she regarded it—and she felt I was somehow
responsible for her in this second chance at happiness.

"What do you do with yourself, Charley?"

"Oh, I watch Cora do her needlework. I get women out
of marriages they thought heaven had gotten them into."

"Don't you ever get lonely?"

"Should I? Haven't I got Cora?"

"Stop it. Charley, this is Victoria. I've met Cora. I know
her. I love her. She's a dear. But for you? Oh, poor Charley."

"Let's talk about something else."

"All right. Read any good books lately?"

"You know. It's nice being here like this with you,
Victoria."

She frowned, a tiny line pulling between her perfect
brows. "Charley, what gives? Why are you suddenly so
attentive?"

"I'm not. I've always loved you, Victoria."

"Don't hurl that word love around like a low score at golf,
Charley. After I got my divorce from Chet—after you got it
for me—I was in a state of—well, upheaval. I needed something. I would have worshipped you, if you'd been nice."

"I couldn't take advantage of you."

"Why not? I wanted you to. I needed somebody. Now, all
of a sudden, you like being here with me."

"I'd like being anywhere with you, Victoria."

Her eyes narrowed slightly. After a moment she said, very softly, "Would you, Charley? Would you? Well, we'll just see about that."

People turned to look at us as we left. I was aware of the whispers; I knew Victoria was. This was what I wanted, and it was almost as though Victoria suspected it.

But that wasn't what bothered me at all. When I walked back into my office at two, Laura was sitting in my judge's chair, awaiting me. She watched me cross the office.

Her voice was chilled. "Who was she?"

I tried to laugh. "Who?"

"The woman you had lunch with."

"You sound like a wife."

"Do I? Well, maybe I do. But there's this to remember, Charley, and you better remember it. I'm in something with you. It's not exactly a game. I'd like to be able to trust you. If I can't trust you . . ."

Her fangs were showing. It was a different Laura. She was not holding checkrein on anything at the moment. Her hazel eyes blazed; there was hatred in those eyes. I felt as though she'd spring across that desk and start clawing at me.

I laughed. For the first time in weeks I felt good.

"Stop laughing, you fool. Chasing around with some woman. Thank God I found out before—"

She jumped up. I caught her in my arms. She beat at me and writhed free. She tried to run and I caught her, dragging her backwards. We lost our balance and fell hard onto the leather couch. She tried to kick and scratch, but I pressed down, holding her so tightly she could hardly breathe.

She kept twisting her head back and forth, her hair falling free, until I mashed my mouth hard over hers. I held her like that until she stopped fighting, until her arms moved around me, and I felt her trembling.

"Oh, Charley. You drive me so crazy. I go wild, and then you kiss me and I can't fight you any more."

"You don't have to fight me."

"Who is she, Charley? She's called twice—before you got back here."

"I hope you told her I'd call back."

"She didn't give me her name, but I know it was she. She kept asking if Charley were back yet."

"I'm sorry, baby. But listen hard. I went to the Brahma today purposely."

"Sure you did."

"Shut up and listen."

"She kept calling."

"I hope she keeps on calling."

"Then you can get along without me. Your kisses may make me all tingly inside—but I don't intend sharing them."

"That was Victoria Haines, Laura. She'll call here often. I want you to play it straight. You're just my secretary as far as Victoria Haines is concerned. And that's all."

She tried to writhe free again. I shoved her back on the couch, hard.

"You wanted in this thing, didn't you? Well, now you've got to trust me. The thing I'm planning—it's going to work only if I'm careful. And cultivating Victoria Haines is part of being careful."

"I don't know what you're talking about."

"Then shut up and listen. My plan needs her. I warn you right now, Laura, we can never be gossiped about—you and I—not even once. If one person suspects we're in love, that's one person too many."

"So you're not even going to think so."

"We've got to be careful, Laura. You know that. Maybe I have got more to win than you—but Cora has a lot of money, and it goes with me."

"What's this Haines woman got to do with it?" She tried to thrust upward and free herself.

"Honey, that's it. She's got everything to do with it. Victoria Haines is going to be the *reason* Cora gets a divorce."

She lay still a moment, her eyes very dark.

"Is Cora going to divorce you?"

"No. But it's got to look as though she had, baby, if we're to stay on top. And that's why you've got to trust me, and that's where Victoria Haines comes in. You've got to trust me."

"Well, I don't."

I pressed my mouth over hers, hard. "You'd better. Starting right now, you'd better."

She writhed beneath me, but she wasn't trying to get free any more.

The blaring ring of the telephone was loud through the offices.

"There she is," Laura said against my mouth. "There she is again."

"Be glad, baby," I told her, "because it has started. Only for right now—we'll let it ring."

When the excitement was enough to burst me, she sat up and pushed her hands through her hair. I could see the smoldering in her eyes. The green was the greenest I had ever seen, and they seemed to be swimming and dry at the same time.

She pushed me away.

"Lord. I can't stand it, Laura. Not like this."

"It's no better for me."

"How long, Laura? How long am I going to have to wait?"

"I don't know, Charley. That's up to you. It's no easier for me. It's worse . . . I never knew it could be like this. I'm having to wait, too."

I stood up and loosened my collar. "I'm going crazy wanting you, being put off."

She stood up, too. Her voice was very low. "If you want to know the truth, Charley, I don't trust you."

"That's great. And why don't you trust me? Because of Victoria? I told you. She means nothing to me."

"It's not Victoria Haines. Not any one thing. It's all of it. We're . . . in something, Charley. As you say, it's for the money, and for your freedom—and for each other. But I stand to lose—"

"What are you talking about?"

"I never had anybody. I'm going to have you . . . but I want to be sure you want me—when it's over."

"Oh, good Lord."

She grabbed my arms, and those green eyes gleamed again. "Do you hear me, Charley? No matter how long we have to wait . . . you're going to want me."

"How long will I have to wait?"

I barely heard her whisper. "That's up to you."

I stared down into her eyes, but I could read nothing in them.

"We can't stampede into this, Laura."

"All right."

"My God. What do you want? Shall I get a gun and shoot her? There's the noise, the bullet, the gun itself. Plenty for them to pick at and work on. I don't think we'd get away with that at all."

"Oh, Charley. I don't mean anything like that." Her face was starkly white, "You know what I want, Charley. I want to belong to you."

I spoke softly, but it seemed like shouting in the silent office. "You can't hurry it," I said. I told her the things I had considered, discarded: a gun, because it would turn up, it could be traced. And a knife. I shuddered when I thought about a knife. I could never use one, even though there was a great deal to say for a knife. Professional killers used them. They figured in crimes of passion. You could use an ordinary kitchen knife, the kind sold in a thousand stores, and it could never be traced to you. But even talking about it in that office, I seemed to see the gush of blood, smell the sick-sweet warmth of it, feel the slime that would not wash off.

"Just one spot of blood on you or your clothing," I said. I shuddered. "That would be enough for a crime lab."

"All right, Charley. I want you to talk yourself out of it. That's what I want."

"But I'm not. I'm talking myself into the one way it can be done—and done so I'm never even suspected."

I paused outside the smart entrance of Maxson-Richards big Main Street department store.

I stood on the walk a moment, thinking about it. Here I was taking the second step toward killing my wife. I was killing Cora right now, right this instant, as surely as if I were choking the breath from her lungs. I had been killing her as I sat in the Brahma, laughing and talking with Victoria Haines where Cora's catty friends could see us together.

People stepped around me, passing me on both sides, hurrying, laughing and talking together. The sun was reflected in the big window, and I stared for a moment at the blaze of the reflected light.

I walked into the store. Women were herding through the aisles. They all looked like Cora, fat, spending money because they didn't have anything else to occupy their minds.

I moved slowly toward the stocking counter. I wanted to buy Cora a pair of stockings. A woman who had been putting some small packages on the shelves behind the case was turning toward me when I changed my mind.

It was a clever thing to buy stockings that were so cheap and so widely sold that they could not be traced anywhere. But was it smart for me to buy them? That fool woman at the counter might remember I'd bought stockings. Even in this enlighted age there's something comic about a man's shopping for his wife.

There was nothing comic about it, but I saw suddenly that I had almost committed my first serious error. I wasn't allowed any errors in this game. It was all right to buy cheap stockings, but not all right for *me* to buy them. A man who bought cheap stockings for his wife would stand out like a boisterous drunk, or a heavy tipper—a man to remember.

I shook my head and turned to walk away.

"Charley. Charley Brower!"

I almost walked into Victoria Haines. Silently I thanked God I hadn't bought the stockings.

"What are you doing in this part of the store?" Victoria said. "You got a girl friend, Charley?"

"Don't you know, Victoria?"

"I wish I knew, Charley. I've been trying to call you. I got to thinking after I left you . . . What you need is to get away from everything—you're too tense. You're worried about something?"

"Me? You're trying to flatter me."

"No. I mean it. What you need is a quiet evening,

Charley. The kind I could fix for you. A cool drink, no friends, no people at all, long-playing records and the lights down low. How does that sound, Charley?"

"Where do I sign up?"

"Tonight, Charley? Could you make it tonight?"

"You forget I'm a married man."

"Yes. Tonight, Charley? About eightish?"

I stood at the window and stared down at Main Street. I did not move until my door opened and Laura hurried in.

"Charley. Here they are."

I turned and she tossed a package from Maxson-Richards on the desk. "Thanks."

I opened the package, wadded the Maxson-Richards paper and tossed it into the waste basket.

"What do you want with them, Charley?"

I opened the box. "Are they cheap?"

She laughed. "They make them by the millions. With built-in runs."

"All right."

I opened my filing cabinet and dropped the stockings inside. I stood there looking down at them. I was thinking, good-by, Cora. This is really good-by, but nobody can ever say I didn't give you every chance.

"Are you comfy, Charley?"

Victoria's voice melted and ran down over me like that goo they spread on sundaes. I lay back on her divan, in the soft bathing of distant indirect lighting, and the soothing whisper of long-playing records. It was all contrived to relax me, but it didn't. I was sweated with impatience. But I went on lying there.

"I'm fine. Fine, Victoria."

"You could have been doing this all this time, Charley. This—and anything else you wanted."

She smoothed her hand along the side of my neck. Her touch was gentle, her fingers barely stroked me, and at first it had been faintly pleasant. Now I felt as though it were ants wearing me raw.

"That's the way it is; a man can't help being blind."

"Are you deaf, too, Charley?"

"No, just dumb." I closed my fingers on her hand, stilling it for a moment. "Why, Victoria?"

"Do you think I want anyone but you, Charley. You think I ever have?"

"I don't know."

"Then you're a fool. I couldn't want anyone else the way I want you. That's why I'm so anxious to tell you . . . I'm going out of town for a week, Charley."

"This is good news?"

"It is—unless you purposely fail to understand, Charley." Her fingers moved along my neck again. "I'm leaving in the morning—for Atlantic City. If you wanted to go away somewhere on business by—day after tomorrow Charley?"

"Gosh, Vic, that sounds fine. I don't know. It's awfully sudden."

"Oh, stop, Charley. You take business trips all the time. I know. You could get away if you wanted to."

"I surely want to, Vic. But I'll have to check."

"You won't regret it, Charley. I promise you won't regret it."

"I already know that."

"Promise?"

I stalled her. I didn't want her too certain I would go. That would make her too careful in her arrangements, too secretive.

That was the last thing I wanted—next to Victoria Haines.

I stopped at the first public pay phone booth on my way home. I got inside, closed the door, listened to the air conditioning start as I dialed. The phone rang ten times. I sweated. Where was Laura? Why wasn't she home?

"Hello." Laura's voice had sleep and warmth in it, the kind of warmth that surged through those wires and got inside me.

"You awake?"

"I am now. What time is it?"

"I don't know. Listen to me. You come up with a sick aunt somewhere. Spread the word around among anybody who might be interested. Pack up. I want you to get ready to fly to New York."

"Why?"

"Because Victoria Haines is going to Atlantic City."

"Maybe I'm still asleep. I don't get it."

"Whenever she leaves town, you and I can leave town. Pack up. I'll see you in the office in the morning."

When Victoria saw me at the train station the following night at eight, something happened in her face. She blushed, looking as confused as a teen-ager.

She stared at first at my face, then at the traveling bag I carried.

"Charley." Her voice was an odd whisper. "Are you taking this train?"

"Aren't you?"

"Yes. I told you I was. But is this—very discreet?"

I grinned at her. "Maybe not. But it's quicker."

For a moment she frowned. She looked about the station. A bevy of her friends was pouring through the doors to bid her good-by.

"You've got to be careful, Charley, please. I'll see you on the train."

Careful was the last thing I wanted to be at the moment, but I didn't say anything about that to Victoria. She had an odd look on her face, almost as if she'd overestimated me, suddenly doubted many things she'd believed about me.

Only one thing annoyed me. There were not many friends of Cora's in the station.

Laura was waiting in her room in the hotel off Times Square. I registered, impatient with the time it took me to sign my name and go through the motions of looking at the room assigned to me.

I knocked on the door, and she threw it open instantly.

She was wearing no make-up, her hair was down around her shoulders, and a bright negligee was caught about her waist.

"Oh, Charley. I didn't expect you so soon."

"Do you throw your door open for every man who knocks like this?"

She laughed, drew me inside. "How was the trip?"

I was looking at her, at her things cast intimately about the room, the scent of her lotions on the dresser.

"Boring," I said. "Victoria was afraid people were going to talk about us. I think she's very disappointed in me. Even when I told her I was changing trains in Philadelphia, had a couple of days' business in New York, she still felt that the people at home wouldn't know that—and were going to talk."

Without moving consciously, we had come close together. I pressed my hands tightly on her negligee.

"I don't want you to go down there to her at all."

"Maybe I won't."

"I wish we could stay like this all the time."

"You do love me?"

"What did you tell Cora?"

"What do I ever tell Cora? That I had business out of town. She'll have to accept it."

"What are people going to think? You and I both gone from the office?"

"What can they think? After seeing the way I scurried away from Victoria in that train station, they won't have time to talk about you."

"What about when you go down there to Victoria?"

"What about right now?"

"Oh, Charley, you drive me crazy."

"You love me?"

"You must know."

"It's not like hearing you say it. Say it."

"I love you, Charley. I'm crazy about you, Charley. I love you, Charley."

"And you're not going to put me off any more?"

"Don't you want to wait—even until you get your coat off?"

I walked up and down outside the huge department store on Fourteenth Street. I kept telling myself that New York was unbelievably huge, the odds against seeing anyone I ever knew were staggering. Yet it seemed to me that

Laura was taking hours over a simple purchase.

We had walked through the bargain basement together and I had pointed out generally the things I wanted. "Keep them simple, and don't buy the dress unless there are at least six other copies of it on the racks. Get the cheapest underthings."

I watched the cars and the people pass me. I sweated.

What difference would it make even if by some crazy, impossible chance someone recognized me outside this store. I had used a phony name on the hotel register. I could swear I hadn't been in New York, certainly not down on Fourteenth Street. Nobody could prove otherwise. Then I knew what was troubling me. It was the possibility of having to lie about it. A murder you might get away with; it was lying that tripped you up.

You had to think of everything when you lied.

"Charley."

I heeled around. Laura was standing there loaded with packages. She looked young and gentle, like a young housewife out shopping for bargains.

"You took long enough."

"Charley. You can't buy even a cheap dress in a hurry. You ought to see the one I bought. I wouldn't want to be found dead in it."

We stared at each other. For an instant, all the sounds of the busy street faded and we were alone in stillness.

She shook her head. She said, "I'm afraid none of these things will be large enough for Cora."

The sense of chill deepened. I looked around, waved at a taxi. My voice sounded odd. "Cora won't care."

I got back to Summit late Sunday night. I hoped I could get quietly into the house and into my bedroom. I was not free of the cloying atmosphere of Victoria Haines. I didn't see how I could face a session with Cora until I had had a few hours' sleep alone.

The lights burned in the front room. I cursed as I let myself in. Cora was lying on the divan, drinking from the mouth of a gin bottle.

She stared up at me. "Did you have a good time?"

"What?"

"You heard me. I said, did you have a good time?"

"Was I supposed to?"

"How was she?"

"Who?"

"Stop trying to play innocent with me."

"I'm not. It's too late to play anything."

"Sure. Too late. And too tired. I hate it when you try to play innocent with me."

"Look. I'm not playing innocent. I am tired. I want to go to bed."

"Go to bed."

"Good night, Cora."

She sat up and threw the bottle. It struck the door at the side of my head. She made a spitting motion toward me. "Victoria Haines."

"What are you talking about?"

"You know what I'm talking about. I'm talking about Victoria Haines in Atlantic City. The Fireside Girl in a Big Hotel. Don't look so offended. I know Victoria Haines was in Atlantic City."

"So?"

"So I don't believe you went to New York. You've got that Atlantic City hotel room tan—especially under your eyes."

"Oh, you're a real comic."

"But you're not?"

"I'm not trying to be."

"With Victoria Haines in Atlantic City. Tell me, what's she like when she bursts out of one of those girdles?"

"I don't know what you're talking about."

She looked around for something else to throw.

"I'm tired of your lying to me!"

"Then don't ask me anything."

"I'm not asking. I'm telling. Oh, I know about you and Atlantic City. A big man on the boardwalk."

"Listen, Cora. Nobody goes to Atlantic City any more. It's grown up, gotten too respectable."

"But you haven't. You wouldn't care. You'd take some no-good to a Sunday School convention if it pleased you."

"All right. You know what I am."

"Oh, do I ever know what you are."

"Why don't you get a divorce, Cora?"

She began to laugh. I felt myself shiver at that laugh. She lay back, shaking her head. "That's why I stayed awake to see you, Charley. I wanted to tell you. If you're trying to force me to divorce you, it won't work. I won't do it. I'm certainly not jealous of Victoria Haines. If only for the sake of your own precious career you might have sense enough to be discreet."

"**B**ut Florida," Laura said. "Why must I fly to Florida?" We were in my office. She was on the divan.

"We've been through it, Laura. It's certainly better. We can't go on like this right here. We can't be seen together anywhere . . . I'm going nuts."

"You want to get rid of me."

"I want to have you, but I told you it could not be a quick thing. The next step is for Cora to start getting a Florida divorce. That's up to you."

"But, Charley, how will we keep word from getting back up here?"

"Why don't you trust me?"

"Because I keep remembering Victoria Haines. Cora might not mind your spending four days with Victoria Haines in Atlantic City, but I cared . . . I didn't think I could stand it. And now you want me to go away for three months. Why can't I go to Reno—it's so much quicker."

"Sure, but it would be out of character. Too risky, and not the sort of place Cora would go. She's supposed to be heartbroken when she finally leaves me."

"And I've got to stay down there for three months?"

"Certainly not. You register in some hotel as Mrs. Charles Brower—"

"That part I like."

"Then when you've established residence, you get a lawyer. I'd send you to one, but it would be better if you found him yourself. Talk around in bars, talk to other women, learn the name of one of the divorce mill grinders. There are plenty of them down there. Get one that's interested in the fee, been in the racket a long time so he's not too particular about where you are between the time you start proceedings and when you go before a judge for the final decree. Let the lawyer set up the case. Any grounds will do, but nothing spectacular. Mental cruelty is perfectly acceptable and covers anything. Don't get yourself talked about, or remembered. When everything is set and the lawyer tells you he doesn't need you until hearing time, you come back up here. Tell him to notify you at the hotel by mail when you are expected to appear. That'll be all right with him."

"I thought I read where they're getting tough on fraudulent residential claims?"

"If they found out, they might make trouble."

"Suppose they found out?"

"Why, they'd throw out the case; it's actually a prosecution offense. But who'll find out? Who wants to find out? Sometimes they find out because the husband or wife blows the whistle. But this is done all the time. When you get the letter telling you that the hearing has been set, you can fly back down there, and you'll appear in the office of some county judge. More than likely you won't even get into his chambers, you'll just appear before one of his clerks. It's that informal. And then it's all over."

"Suppose somebody up here finds out?"

"They won't."

"The lawyer might notify you of the bill of complaint?"

"He won't. That's one of the gimmicks in a Florida divorce. When you see this lawyer the first time, you simply tell him my address is at the moment unknown, that you'll supply it later. This will tell him plenty. He'll publish the notice of divorce proceedings as required by law, but he'll have them printed in the most obscure country newspaper he can find. It's done all the time. The divorce takes three months—and I swear to you, Laura, by the time the notice of her divorce is sent here to me Cora will be out of the way. As far as anybody will know Cora and I will be divorced."

"You swear it, Charley?" She was trembling in my arms.

I held her close. "It'll be all over, and if we work it right, nobody will ever suspect anything."

"But I'll be gone for so long."

"When it's over, baby, we'll be on top of the world—together."

"But down there by myself—when will I see you?"

I laughed. "That's easy. You'll see me the first time Victoria Haines leaves town."

But a week later I was in Florida. I hurried from a plane at the Tampa Airport and inquired about limousine service to the St. Petersburg beaches. When I was told it might take longer than two hours to make the twenty-five mile trip, I hired a cab.

We raced across the bridge, but it seemed to me we were crawling. I could not stay away from Laura any more. Her letters, brief and unsatisfactory, left me hungry and despairing.

It was the middle of the afternoon when I got a motel room at Passagrille Beach. I registered as Richard Smith, Richmond, Virginia. This Richard Smith was really getting around.

I was only a few blocks from Laura, but I couldn't barge in at her place in the middle of the afternoon. She was playing the role of the wife driven to divorce. She would play it to the nth degree, I knew, and I wasn't going to spoil it by playing a reunion scene for the loafers.

I stalked about inside my room. An oblong crib with bath and indented space for cooking on a small stove, it was furnished with a pay-TV set, a club chair and a daybed. The walls pushed in on me. Though Laura was so near, both of us were so alone.

I went outside and stepped into a pay booth. Through the glass sides. I saw people playing shuffleboard, bridge, or swimming. Girls sprawled, glistening with suntan lotion, on bright beach towels. The palm trees were motionless in the brassy, airless afternoon. Far across the white beach I saw the Gulf lying glass-smooth. In the hot afternoon, with the laughter beating at the glass walls of the booth, it was hard to think of murder.

It was easy to think of Laura.

Finally she answered. My heart leaped at the excitement in her tone. "Charley. For goodness sake, Charley. Where are you?"

"About a block from you."

"Charley! You're teasing."

"No. I'm here. I couldn't stand it any more."

"What are you doing a whole block away? Get over here, as fast as you can."

"No. I've got to be careful, Laura. Just as careful as you must be. I don't want people talking about you."

"Well, this is fine. Torment me. When will I see you?"

"As soon as it gets dark. Leave a Girl Scout cookie burning in the window."

A pause. "Charley . . ."

"What?"

"Have you done it yet?"

"No. Not yet. It's too soon."

"You—are going to?"

"Don't you trust me?"

"I've been so lonely down here. Too much time to think, I guess."

"You want to back out?"

"Charley, you know better than that."

I went along her street, feeling the sense of expectancy mounting. I heard people in the other apartments talking, eating, listening to television. The place Laura had chosen was gleaming white with two wings jutting along a grassy patio. The wings faced each other. I paused for a moment, in the darkness beyond the front entrance, looking along both wings. I did not want someone sitting in a concealed deck chair watching me move like a thief searching for Laura's apartment number.

Both wings appeared empty. I exhaled and moved away from the darkness. Hers was Number Fifteen; it would be across the grass patio.

I looked both ways and then walked out into the beginning of moonlight. I wanted to appear cagey, as if I owned a part of the place at least. I had taken less than four steps into the patio when a door opened behind me, and light sprayed across me and I stopped still.

"Friend. Just a sec, friend."

A man strolled through the door, leaving it open. He crossed the cement walk and stepped out onto the grass.

I told myself I was feeling panic out of all proportion to the importance of this thing. But I could not escape the sensation that something had gone wrong, would go all wrong. I asked myself coldly what difference it made if this man looked at me, remembered me, a thousand miles from Summit. I couldn't answer that. But I couldn't stop the fluttering of panic either.

He stood looking at me.

He was tanned a travel-folder brown and I got the feeling he had gotten it hurriedly, and that he had worked hard for this tan because it had to be just right, the way his black hair was waved correctly, and his mustache was trimmed to precise length.

I reminded myself I had nothing against his oily good looks or the fact that he could afford to bask all day in the sun. What I disliked was the knowing leer in his dark eyes and the way his mouth twisted. It was as if he told me I was in here stealthily and that I despised being caught like this, pinned in the light from his doorway. I shook the thought away. It had to be my conscience. What business was it of his if I came to visit a woman across the patio?

Still, if anything else went wrong, he could testify I had been down here in Florida to visit Laura, only her name was Mrs. Charles Brower. The last thing I wanted was for anyone to think I ever visited Cora down here after she finally went away from Summit for the divorce Laura and I were getting in her name.

"Got a match?" he said.

His voice was low, modulated. Ordinarily, I wouldn't have given a character like that a second thought. But I didn't want him nibbling at me in the next few weeks.

"No," I said. "I'm sorry. Uh, maybe you can help me?"

"Sure. You looking for somebody?"

"Yes. A Mr. Smith. Mr. Richard Smith."

He shrugged. "Might be somebody in the motel by that name. Wouldn't know."

"Well, is this the Marlin Motel?"

"No, friend. You got the wrong place. It's about a block north."

"That's it, then. I've got the wrong place."

"You sure have. You don't have a match?"

I shook my head again, turned and walked back toward the darkened entrance, where I paused and watched him.

He stayed out on the patio for a long time. He seemed to be watching something in the sky, maybe the moon. Finally he went back inside his room and closed the door.

Sweating, I went across to the other wing and walked rapidly along it, hugging the wall. I found Number 15. It was directly across from Oily's room. I rapped faintly.

After a moment, Laura opened the door. I pushed past her and closed it behind me. Before I even spoke to her, I crossed and pulled the venetian blind shut so hard the slats vibrated.

She was wearing a sheer negligee, something she had bought for me. She was standing in the middle of the room, frowning faintly. I went to her, pulled her against me. For a long time we stood holding each other. She whispered. "I've missed you, missed you, missed you."

"Who's the gigolo across the patio?" I said.

She tilted her head back. "What an old-fashioned expression," was all she said.

"He's an old-fashioned type. He looked me over good."

"He doesn't matter, darling. He's nobody. You're all tense. You don't even act glad to see me."

I caught her so tightly she could scarcely breathe. "I am glad, though. I can't help the tenseness. It's the business I'm in."

"Poor Charley."

"Don't say that. You sound like Cora. Or Victoria Haines."

"God forbid. Let me look at you, Charley. It's been so long."

"Let me look at you."

She did. We forgot the man across the patio, and Cora and Victoria Haines, and anything else beyond that locked door. It was worth coming to Florida for. It was worth everything. . . .

I left Laura at two that morning. I was almost at the Marlin Motel when I paused in the shadows. A gray 1950 Plymouth with an Indiana license tag was parked at the curb. I took out a screwdriver I had bought, stepped out behind

the car, knelt against the bumper. It took less than two minutes to remove the license plate and shove it in my jacket
pocket with the screwdriver.

I straightened up then and walked quietly through the
shadows. The Marlin was completely dark and silent.

I stopped off at the office on my way home from the airport, and added the license plate to the other things accumulating in my files. For a long time I stood looking at the
things I had accumulated: dress, underthings, stockings,
and now a license plate from an Indiana car.

Cora came into my bedroom while I was undressing
for bed.

"What a delightful surprise," she said. "At first I thought
it was a burglar."

"You're not that lucky."

"No. I'm not very lucky, am I?"

"You can always get a divorce, Cora."

"Did you hear the news?"

"What news?"

"About Gulick Williams?"

Gulick Williams was a friend of mine who'd been elected
judge of the circuit court in the last elections. "No," I said.
"I haven't seen a newspaper."

"Doesn't Victoria give you time to read the papers?"

"What's this about Victoria now?"

"Nothing. Just that she was out of town this week. Isn't
that a delightful coincidence?"

"Whether it's delightful or not it's just a coincidence." I
stepped into my pajamas. "What about Gulick?"

"He died. A heart attack."

I sat down on the bed. Gulick was a year younger than I
was; when your friends begin dropping dead around you,
you start to worry.

"You should be more careful about the way you carry on
with Victoria Haines. You should have more respect for
your position. People are talking."

I didn't tell her nothing could please me more.

Mike Welch grinned and got up from behind his desk when I walked into his office on the used-car lot. He came around the desk with his hand outstretched. As always he wore a felt hat and had a cigar in his mouth. Tufts of prematurely gray hair showed under his hat. He was in his thirties but had a rugged, lined face that appeared much older.

"Counsellor! Long time no. Come on, some of you bums, get up and give the counsellor a chair."

There were three or four salesmen in his office. I had seen a couple more out on the lot as I came through. Mike's lot was the largest in Summit. He was a sharp operator, a dangerous man to do business with unless you understood mechanics and loan-shark financing. Few people understand both. Yet he did a big trade.

I shook hands with Mike, glancing at the salesmen still loitering inside the smoke-filled office.

"All right, all right, you guys. Get some money coming in. What do I pay you for?"

We all knew Mike Welch never paid a salary to anybody except the girls in his finance office and the men who washed the cars and swept out the lot. But the salesmen grinned and left. They had it good with Mike Welch. In Summit when anybody thought of used cars, they thought of the Crazy Irishman. That was the way he advertised himself in every newspaper and on the radio and television. If you believed his advertising, he was trying to give his cars away, only the Federal Trade Commission wouldn't let him. Just the same, he kept that name in everybody's mind. Hadn't I thought of him first when I decided it was time to buy the car?

"Sit down. Sit down. Let me fix you a drink." Mike squatted in the swivel chair behind his desk and took a fifth from the bottom drawer. I shook my head. He shrugged and replaced the bottle. "What you need, Counsellor?

You've come to the right place, whatever it is."

"I need a little information, Mike." This was not true. What I wanted was to buy a used car. But I was not going to buy it from Mike Welch. It had to come from farther away than he got his cars.

"You need it, you name it," he said. He struck fire to his cigar, watching me. "How about a little party, Counsellor? You know I been promising to fix you up with something nice and friendly. You done me a big service. I don't forget things like that. What would you like? Blonde? Brunette? Old? Young? They all come to me sooner or later to buy a car, and I haven't met one yet that didn't want to try it out on the Pig tracks. Once out there, they want to test the back seat. Once they been in the back seat with Mike Welch, they're hooked. I tell you, I don't know what's happening to the younger men. I'm worried about the future of this here country. Young fellows not like you and me. I tell you I got young salesmen on the lot, good-looking lads in their twenties, ought to be all full of prime. They get one woman a day, they've had it. Lie around like a sick dog for a couple of days afterwards. Man, I never could have built a business like this if I didn't have more to offer than that. I got pushed into the corner the other night—no salesmen on the lot except me—I had to take on three different dames between seven and ten o'clock. Would you believe that, Counsellor?"

"Why not? You want me to, don't you?"

He laughed. "Counsellor, I'm in your debt. Anything I can do."

Mike had gotten into a serious jam about a year before and had come to me, sweating blood. It was the only time I ever knew him to forget to talk about women and his prowess with them. He had bought a couple of stolen cars and the FBI got him. He knew he was slated for the Federal pen. He kept yelling that a reputable dealer couldn't help getting rooked once in a while.

We went to court, and the only thing that saved Mike was that I was able to prove that one of the government's witnesses was so unsavory a character that his evidence was no good in any court. Through a lack of prosecution, Mike had been released.

"Mike," I said, watching him, "I don't need any blondes or redheads today—"

"That's where you're wrong, man. Everybody needs a blonde or a redhead. Every day. If every man got himself a blonde or redhead every day, you know what? There'd be no wars, no ulcers and no coronary attacks. Trouble comes when a man forgets what the good Lord put him here on earth for. Let me give you a couple of numbers so hot they singe the phone lines, Counsellor."

"I want something hotter than that. I want the name of the guy who runs the hot car ring you deal with."

I had socked it to him hard and he sat back looking as though I had struck him.

His cigar had burned out. He removed it from his mouth, looked at it distastefully, slapped it back.

"Counsellor, I don't know what to say."

"His name."

"Now, look here."

"No, you look here. This is us, Mike. Me and you. You think I thought you were innocent when I got you off? Don't make me laugh. Those FBI boys had you by the short hairs—"

"And they'd get me again if I fooled around with any hot car ring—"

"Look, Mike, I'm in a hurry. Now deal from top of the deck, or the next time somebody blows the horn on you you can get yourself another lawyer."

"Now, Counsellor—"

"That's the way it is. You're always talking about owing me something. Well, now I need to know the name of this guy."

"Good Lord, Counsellor. If anything happened to this boy, and they ever found out I had breathed his name—even in my sleep—they'd flay me, clothes and all."

"Nothing is going to happen to him. I need to know the top boy, because I've got a case that is going to need some tricky work. I may not even get in touch with him. But I want his name."

Back in my office I put through the long-distance call to the name Mike had given me. It wasn't easy to get through to this boy, even when I had his personal telephone number. Three men wanted to know where I got that number before I could talk with the big shot.

We spent a long fifteen minutes sparring. I told him I wanted to buy a three-year-old used car, either gray or black, and not freshly painted.

Five times he told me I was crazy, that I had the wrong number. But I was patient, and I mentioned a good price.

"What did you say your name was?"

"Richard Smith," I told him.

"Yeah. That's a good American name. How do I know you ain't trying to spring a trap on me?"

"On the telephone? Deny you talked to me. You don't have the car I want, forget it. But if you do, you deliver it to the All-Hours Garage here in Summit. Leave it in the name of Richard Smith, then send the claim check to Richard Smith, General Delivery, in Wyattstown."

"Suppose I did that? How do I get this money?"

"Cash. The best way there is. By telegraph. Give me any address and I'll send it."

He thought that over for a long time. Finally he told me to send the money to the Western Union office in Richmond, Virginia, to Lois Osgood. I wrote that down and that was the last time we talked together. . . .

The next afternoon, I attended the funeral of Gulick Williams with Cora. Every attorney in the state was there. The Governor spoke a few words. The smell of the flowers was oppressive. I thought about Victoria Haines, the way she spilled out of those foundation garments, the oppressive sweetness, the way she crowded you every moment you were near her. I glanced at Cora, thinking she wasn't the worst thing that could happen to you.

I was astonished to see Victoria there among the mourners. It had not occurred to me she might know Gulick Williams. She was in the Governor's party, and she looked smooth and correct in black.

Cora saw me looking at Victoria and I heard her sigh.

During the lengthy services, I could feel Victoria glancing at me. I did not look her way again. I knew that people were whispering. Talk had built up in the past few weeks. They were pitying Cora. Mentally I invited any one of them to walk a mile in my sandals and then criticize me. Though it was a laugh to think I'd ever spend five minutes in Victoria's company when I didn't have to. But what these gossips didn't know wasn't going to hurt me.

I was very upset by Gulick's sudden death. That sounds senseless, being moved by a natural death when I was thinking how soon I was going to kill my wife. But I couldn't help it. Gulick had been a fine man, with a brilliant career ahead of him.

We drove home in silence.

"Victoria," Cora said, "looked very sleek. I didn't know she was a friend of the Governor."

"Neither did I."

"My. She doesn't tell you much about herself. What's the matter, don't you talk much?"

I pulled into the driveway, hearing the tires scrape on the gravel. I stopped the car. Cora started to get out. I put my hand on her arm.

"Cora, I've something I want to tell you."

"You don't have to tell me anything. I know everything there is to know. Much more than I want to know."

"No, this is something else. Something different. This whole business with Victoria. I admit I got mixed up with her. I mean, she threw it at me—it was a mistake. She talks too much. She's too much trouble. The whole thing was wrong."

"I could have told you that."

"I had to find it out for myself."

"What I want to know is, what's par for the course, Charley? How many of these women do you have to make a fool of yourself over before you grow up?"

I stared out the window. "I don't know, Cora. That's up to you."

"Up to me? What are you talking about?"

"I don't know, Cora. I'm tired. I'd like to get away. This sudden death of Gulick has upset me—"

"Getting old, dad?"

"Something like that. Anyhow, if you'd go away with me we could have—a second honeymoon."

Her smile was bitter. "I think you're too worn out for any honeymoons."

I shrugged. "We were happy once, Cora."

"Yes. But I can hardly remember that far back."

"You don't want to try?"

"I try all the time. I'm the only one who ever tries at all." She wiped tears from her eyes. "Then when you find out another tramp is just a tramp and want to run away—I'm supposed to leap eagerly at the chance."

"All right," I said. "Forget it."

She sat there a moment. Finally she sighed. "Where would you like to go, Charley?"

"Would you like to fly to Nassau?"

"You know I don't like to fly."

"A boat then."

"You know a boat makes me ill. I'm sorry, Charley. I'm afraid I'm just a stay-at-home."

"You wouldn't want to do it," I said, as though I had just thought of it. "But remember our honeymoon?"

She laughed. "In that old car of yours. We made a tour. Was it three states before it broke down?"

"I couldn't help it. I was broke." I touched her arm. "We could do it again, Cora. You and I, just driving around. It might save us."

"Oh, Charley." She burst out crying. "Would you, Charley? Just you and I? Oh, I'd love that."

I stared at the top of her head. I had known she was going, but what I hadn't known was that she would be so eager. This was just what she wanted, and she couldn't wait to get started.

Cora spent the rest of the afternoon and most of the evening talking on the telephone. Too many people had come—in a friendly manner—to cut her pins from under her with stories about Victoria Haines and me. When she called, she never mentioned Victoria's name or what they may have said to her. Usually she was just calling, she said, to cancel an engagement in the immediate future since she would not be in town. "Charley and I are going away for an extended trip. He insisted I go with him. Just wouldn't take no for an answer."

I sat around with her, letting her stroke my shoulders or pat my hair as she walked past me, humming. I never wanted a drink so badly in my life. But I didn't dare have one; what was ahead was too tricky.

About eight-thirty Cora's closest friend came over from next door. Edie Myers was about three years older than Cora.

She and Cora walked all over the house discussing the trip Cora and I were taking. They searched in closets, rummaged through cedar chests, drank coffee in the kitchen, while making lists of all the things Cora should remember to take with her.

About ten I decided Cora and her pal were going to sit up all night. I was drawn so fine their voices twanged my nerves like guitar strings. I walked out of the kitchen.

Edie looked up at me, one of those bless-you smiles wreathing her face. "I'm so glad for you, Charles. For you and Cora."

"Sure," I said. "Maybe Cora and I haven't gotten along too well here lately, but with some luck—everything is going to be different."

Cora's head jerked up. I saw the hurt in her eyes, as if she wished I hadn't said that.

But I had had to say it.

By one A.M. Cora was finally asleep in her room. I listened at her door. Her breathing was deep, as though she were really sleeping soundly for the first time in weeks.

Something kept nagging at me. Through my mind ran the thought that it was still not too late to call a halt.

I had to remind myself of Laura down there in that Florida motel and how at last I would be free to have her.

I looked about the house; I was not going to lose any of this. I was going to keep it all. The only difference was that Cora would not be in it—the biggest single improvement since solid oak flooring.

I walked along the hall, dialed a cab company and spoke as softly as I could ordering a taxi to pick me up at the corner of Forest Drive and 65th.

I left all the lights out, and softly closed the front door behind me.

There was a rising breeze, loud in the elms, that flipped the leaves along the gutter. The whole street was dark. I stayed on the walk and moved swiftly to the corner. Somewhere in the darkness a dog barked.

I waited about five minutes and then the taxi swung off 65th and stopped for me. I gave him my office address downtown and sat back, suddenly chilled in the warm cab.

I went up the elevator in the still building. The whine of the cables and the clink of chains were loud in the shaft.

I let myself into my office and snapped on my desk lamp. For a moment I paused, looking at everything, thinking how much it had cost Cora, how much I had cost her. And I learned right there that it's one thing to think about killing someone, to wish her dead, and it's something else to know the moment has come. You can't turn back, not if you want the things you've told yourself you want. But you know from this moment you are no longer Charles Brower, attorney at law. You're a killer. A murderer. It doesn't matter whether you get away with it or not. It doesn't matter what anyone else in the world thinks about you. It's what you know yourself.

Angrily I pulled open the filing cabinet and gathered up the things I had been accumulating there, the dress, the underthings, the license plate, the stockings, the screwdriver. I put them in a large flat envelope and got out of there. . . .

A nineteen-year-old boy was the only attendant on duty at the All-Hours Garage. He was sleepy, barely looked at the flimsy disguise I had worn for his benefit: my reading glasses, my hat turned down so my face was in shadows.

I handed him the parking receipt I had picked up at the Wyattstown General Delivery. He stared at it a moment, and I felt my pulses quicken.

Then he nodded. "Oh, yes, Mr. Smith. It's the fifty Studebaker Champion. Right?"

"Right."

He consulted a chart. "We serviced the car, sir, filled it with gas, oil and water. Put a sticker on the door."

"Oh. Thanks."

He brought the car and it was exactly what I had hoped for. It was a gunmetal gray, apparently in good shape, but a car that you would not remember two minutes after you passed it.

I tipped him, paid him for the service and parking charges, and drove out. The car handled nicely. I drove slowly until I found a dark, uninhabited block on the edge of town.

I stopped the car and took off the old license plate. I threw it as far as I could into a vacant lot, then I replaced it with the Indiana license plate I had stolen in Florida. If they ever did try to trace this thing—car, license plate and title—somebody was going to have a fit.

I drove home, turning off the lights before I reached my driveway. I went as quietly as the car would purr into the darkness beside the carport.

Before I went into the house I got some water from the hose and washed off the service sticker. That was one little item I wasn't going to forget.

I went into the house carrying the clothes. My arms felt leaden, and my legs seemed watery. I was afraid they were not going to support me. I placed the clothing on the floor outside Cora's room and cautiously opened the door, stepping to the side to stand in the darkness for a moment. In the stillness I could hear that barking dog again.

"Cora," I said, keeping my voice very low.

I could see her now, a lump under the sheets on the bed. She stirred restlessly and I held my breath, watching.

"Cora. You awake?"

She rolled her head again and I moved forward stealthily. I was trembling all over. My hands shook.

I stood beside her bed and gently lifted the covers, pulling them over her shoulders and patting them tightly along her body. When she started to writhe, the covers would pin her arms against her, and she would roll herself up in them.

I moved up beyond her head and stood looking down at her for a moment. Good-by, Cora. I had despised her for years, but right then I pitied her, because in a moment it was going to be over.

I lifted one of her pillows, folded it slightly and placed it down over her face. I moved fast and roughly then. Closing my arms around the pillow, I held it as tightly over her face as I could press it, thrusting down with all the weight of my body.

She hurled herself upward and I let her make a half turn to the right, fighting like a hooked shark; then I wrenched her back the other way and her body got tangled in the bed clothes.

She writhed and twisted for a long time. My leaden arms got weak and I was afraid she would fight free. I didn't know it would take so long for her to suffocate. It was as if time stopped and she fought to live. Her body rolled back and forth. She tried to fight her arms free. I heard the loud sobbing gasps as she tried to breathe through the pillow.

Finally it ended. Her movements weakened and her hands twitched and then there was no movement at all.

I flopped forward across her. I don't know how long I stayed there. She was completely still, a lifeless mass on the bed.

Suddenly sobs wracked me. I sobbed, not knowing what I was crying for. Maybe for Cora, maybe for all the miserable unhappy people on earth, but mostly for me.

For Charles Brower, murderer.

At last I got up and staggered into her bathroom. I was sick.

When I came out I was weak, shaking all over, and just knowing I had to touch Cora's body again, had to dress her in the cheap nameless clothes I'd bought for her, made my stomach tighten into knots all over again.

Somehow I did it. Sweat dripped from me and my fingers shook, reacted clumsily. But I got the ugly underthings, stockings and dress on her. How Cora was going to hate being found dead in these things.

I packed her a suitcase, carried it down and put it in her Buick. Then I came back and carried her downstairs. She hung limply, her arms dragging on the floor. Twice I almost dropped her.

I laid her out on the backseat of the Studebaker. She looked as though she were asleep, only there was no pulse, no heartbeat, no life. I kept telling myself I was free of Cora.

I looked at my watch. It was almost three A.M. Two hours since Cora had finally fallen asleep. It seemed as long as half a lifetime. I had less than two hours to put Cora's car in a storage garage and get out of this neighborhood before daylight.

I felt a quickening of that old panic. Time was something you could not plan in advance, not in a thing like this. I ran back into the house, looked around to be sure I hadn't left anything behind. Then I locked the back doors, making certain that Edie Myers wouldn't drop in before I got back.

I was almost at the front door when the bell started shrilling. It was like the side of a hand across my neck. The sound clattered in my brain. I stared at the front door.

It took me almost a full minute to realize it was the telephone.

I tried to make up my mind whether to answer it or not. Who'd be calling me at three in the morning? Had Edie Myers heard me moving around over here and decided we had burglars? It was better not to answer it at all. Then I thought of Laura. Maybe something has gone wrong. I had to answer it.

I raced toward it, afraid now it would stop ringing before I could lift the receiver.

"Hello." My voice was so shaken and breathless I hardly recognized it.

"Charley. Darling. Did I wake you?"

"Who is this?"

"Why, Victoria, honey."

Impatience flooded through me. That marshmallow sauce in her voice made me sweat. I gripped the receiver, wanting to slap it back in its cradle. "Good lord, Vic, it's three in the morning."

"Yes. I know. I just got home. I think you'll be glad I called you."

"I'm glad. Good night, Vic."

Her laugh stopped me. "You better hear me out."

"All right. What is it?"

"I must see you at once."

"It's impossible, Victoria. I'm going out of town. Right away."

"Without me. Why angel, you can't."

"Angel, I'm going to."

"You better forget it and come over here."

"I can't talk any more."

"Not even about Gulick Williams' job?"

It was as if she had hit me in the small of the back. I toppled against the wall, and gagged. I was afraid I was going to be sick again.

"I just left the Governor, darling. We had a wonderful talk. And they mentioned you."

I still could not speak. There was a bitter sickness in my mouth.

"Did you hear me, Charley? They talked about you for Circuit Judge in the Fifth District—two years of Gulick's unexpired term."

I made a sound in my throat. I don't know what Victoria thought I said. She laughed. I barely heard her. I was standing there in the darkness seeing Cora writhing and fighting me on that bed, fighting to live, and suddenly it was as if she had been fighting for me instead of against me. She had been fighting to stay alive so that I could have that judgeship—something I wanted with all my heart.

"You're not the only one they mentioned, or anything like that, darling. I wouldn't want you to think it was that simple. But I know the right people, Charley—the right people, and the right things to say. Think of it! Did you ever think I would be able to do something like this for you?"

"No."

"Of course you didn't. You just thought I was good for taking to bed. Isn't that what you thought, Charley, you naughty boy."

"Yes."

She laughed. "I'm good for that, too."

I was thinking about that appointment to Gulick's unexpired term on the bench, one of those foolish, impossible things that just could happen. The right politics, being in the right place at the right time.

Oh, I was in the right place, all right.

"Don't you think you better get over here, Charley? There's so much we've got to talk about."

"I can't."

"Charley. I think you better be nice to me—nicer than you have been. A chance like this won't come again."

"No."

"You can have that job, Charley. The right word from me, and it's yours. But I'm not just making you a present of a plum like that, Charley."

"No."

"No. You're so right. So come on over."

"What about—Cora?"

She laughed. "What about Cora? I think you're going to divorce Cora, Charley. I've thought so for a long time. I was suspicious of you from that first day you started paying too much attention to me in public. You were using me. Using me to make Cora lose face, force her to divorce you. Oh, I knew, Charley. I wasn't born yesterday. I'm not stupid. I knew you were using me, but I didn't mind, as long as I was getting—well, part of what I wanted from you. And as long as there was a chance that when you were free—well, we'll talk about that, Charley."

Slowly, the blood began to move in my veins again and my pulse speeded slightly. Maybe there was a chance out of this, maybe I could still have this impossible prize.

If I could make Victoria believe that I was going to divorce Cora, stall her long enough to finish my plan and return to Summit, I might still win everything.

"Cora and I—we are getting a divorce, Victoria. But that's for you alone to know. If you repeat it—"

"Darling! Why should I? Just now when there must not be a breath of scandal if you are to get that appointment. I'll be discretion itself. That's why I want to see you now in the dark of night so no one will suspect. I can help you get that appointment—I can get it for you—but we'll have to be more careful than we have been until the Governor makes his announcement."

"You must forgive me, Victoria. About tonight. Cora and I—well, we're taking a trip. I promise you, it won't be much longer. But I can't see you until I get back."

"Charley, I don't know if I like this or not."

"Vic, you've got to trust me." The telephone receiver was sweat-slicked now.

Her voice got throaty. "I don't trust you. I never have. That's what makes you so exciting to me. I don't think I ever will trust you." Her voice ran like gobs of hot chocolate. "But when I get you—I won't let you out of my sight."

I replaced the receiver and stood there, shivering.

I looked at my watch. I wiped the perspiration from my face. I could not get downtown, leave the Buick, get back out here before daylight. It was impossible.

I stared about the darkened house, feeling trapped. Then I remembered how I'd gotten the Studebaker.

I flashed on a small table lamp and found Mike Welch's home number. I dialed, listened to it ring. Everything was breaking for me. When the chips were down, I began to think clearly. I was going to get out of this all right.

Judge Charles Brower.

"Hello. Mike Welch speaking. If this is some woman, hang up, you got the wrong number."

"Mike. This is Charles Brower."

His voice chilled. "Oh, hello, Counsellor."

"Mike. That name I asked you about."

"Oh Lord, Counsellor. So I'm not worried enough about giving you his phone number, you have to call me up in the middle of the night to remind me?"

"All right. You can rest better. I can tell you now what I wanted with him. I've got a Buick out here. My wife's car. This year's model. A real lemon, but insured to the front fender. I want you to send somebody out here right away to pick it up. I want it to go to your lot—and from there to our friend."

"You going to try to collect insurance?"

"What else?"

"I better tell you, Counsellor—"

"You don't have to tell me anything. You got a couple boys down at your lot, haven't you? Send one of them out to my place right away. I'll be out there waiting."

"Counsellor—"

"Do this one thing for me, Mike, and we're quits."

He was silent a long moment. Finally, he spoke coldly.

"As you say, Counsellor. If you're sure this washes us up. I'll have a boy out there in twenty minutes."

While I waited for Mike's boy to show up, I removed Cora's suitcase from her Buick, put it in the back seat of the Studebaker with her. I couldn't risk putting her in the trunk. If my plan were to succeed, her body had to be completely free of bruises or marks that might arouse suspicion. In a way, I was glad I didn't have to subject her to that last indignity.

I went back to the Buick, kept busy removing all the traces of her that I could find from her car.

A taxi stopped out front and a youth in coveralls came along the drive.

He saw me standing in the darkness. He did not appear to think anything was unusual. "This the car I'm supposed to pick up, mister?"

I told him it was. I stood there, watched him back down the drive and go away along Forest Drive. Then I got into the Studebaker.

I crossed the state line, going west, just before daybreak.

You'll never be so lonely as on a highway driving with a corpse on the back seat. I drove steadily, watching for every traffic sign and obeying them all. If a speed maximum called for forty-five, I stayed at an even forty, taking no chances on an eager patrolman with a faulty speedometer.

I watched the back mirror. Everything depended on how little attention I attracted in the next forty-eight hours—not so much on whether I got away with this part of the business, as to what would happen to me later on.

My hands tightened on the wheel. This was the biggest part of the gamble, and yet I was not as worried about this moment as the days that must follow when I did get away with this. If I did.

I could relax about what I was doing right now. Either I succeeded now, or the whole plan was shot and I was on the way to the electric chair. . . .

The bright glare of the morning sun was painful to my eyes, which burned from lack of sleep. I kept wiping at them with the back of my hand.

A state patrolman passed me going east, his car gliding at sixty, gaze intent on something ahead. Some poor devil in trouble, I thought.

I had no time to waste worrying about anyone else. I could not keep my thoughts away from Victoria's call. What an impossible thing, and yet I knew I could have had that judgeship. I could have had it. In the rear-view mirror I stared for a moment at Cora's placid face. I looked at her until my eyes misted over.

I jerked my gaze back to the highway. It was much more crowded now. Cars raced past me, suddenly loud, and then the silence that followed when they pulled away. I was completely alone, completely cut off from communication with any of those people. I was alone on the earth. Alone with my thoughts, and with Cora.

There had never been a moment since my first year in high school when I had decided on law as a career that I had not daydreamed myself into the seat of a judge, bringing a new wisdom and fairness to it, and then in the chambers of the United States Senate.

Charles Brower, murderer.

My head ached all the way to the nape of my neck. I passed restaurants, drive-ins, truck stops. All of them advertized the best coffee on the road. I glanced back at Cora, at that placid look on her face. I did not stop.

On the seat beside me was the pad and pencil. Before I pulled out of the yard I had carefully noted the mileage. I had been driving about six hours now; I still had half a tank of gas. I told myself this was a good omen. It was a break, the little car got excellent mileage.

I didn't stop for lunch. By three o'clock in the afternoon I knew I'd have to have gas. This was the test. I had driven almost five hundred miles; I had seven hundred more to go.

I swung off the westbound highway on a broad artery stretching north. I slowed, pulled off my jacket and lovingly covered Cora, tucking it about her throat and shoulders. She looked as if she were sleeping. I could even believe it. The smile on her face was almost smug.

Sweating, I pulled into a filling station—a busy one with six pumping islands.

"Yes, sir?"

"Fill it up," I said, keeping my voice low.

"Regular or ethyl?"

"Regular's fine."

He glanced over my shoulder. He lowered his voice and grinned. "Really sleeping, ain't she?"

"Yes. We've been driving a long way."

"See you folks are from Indiana. Been down in Florida?"

"Yes."

He went back to the pumps, started the gas and then checked under the hood. I watched him, feeling the sweat break out over my face. I felt greasy with sweat.

I looked around helplessly. It was as if that gas hose chained me to this station, as though any moment that boy was going to realize that Cora would not stay asleep with the noise of the cars, the hood slamming down, the voices of the other attendants.

My gaze struck a pyramid of red gasoline cans. I stared at them a moment, then I got out, walked over and picked up one.

I brought it back to the pump island where the attendant was just removing the hose from my gas tank.

"Will you fill this up for me?" I said. "We want to try to make it home by tomorrow morning. Maybe I won't be able to find a filling station open late tonight."

The boy shrugged. "Want to sell you the gas tank, mister, but you can make it to any place in Indiana before morning—no trouble at all from here."

I bit at the anger that welled in my mouth. I said, "I don't know. Tired as I am. I may have to stop for a while."

He was filling the can for me. "Your wife don't drive?"

"No."

"Well, you got plenty gas now." He stared at me. "You look like you could use a rest all right, mister."

In Missouri that night, my headlights picked out the name of the creek I was crossing. Turnback River. Faintly, I wondered how it had gotten its name, but mostly I saw that

I was alone on the dark highway. I stopped, backed up.

I got out of the car, weariness making my knees tremble. I found half a dozen stones. Then I took Cora's suitcase out of the back seat and put the stones in with the clothing I had packed for her. I closed the case, carried it out on the small bridge and dropped it. I heard the splash and then silence washed in over me.

Far down the road behind me I saw the pinpoints of headlamps. I ran back to my car, got in, drove away.

The highway wavered in front of me. It was early morning and the darkness pressed against the car windows. My eyes were heavy and dry, and felt scaly.

I awoke suddenly when my front tire struck the shoulder on the left side of the highway.

I twisted the wheel, pulled back on the road. Behind me I saw headlights. If it was a state highway patrol, they'd stop me for drunken driving. For the next few miles I was wide awake. My head bobbed and I felt the car weaving. A horn was blaring behind me. I forced my eyes open. I was on the wrong side of the road. The horn went on blaring even when I pulled back on the right lane.

I slowed down, so fatigued I did not care. If it was cops, at least it was all over.

A man leaned out of the window of the car when it pulled up beside me.

He yelled, "You better stop for a coffee break, bud. You're going to kill yourself or somebody else driving in your sleep."

I pulled into a graveled drive-in at the edge of a town. I stopped in the darkness and glanced at Cora.

I almost staggered going into the diner.

The waitress was blonde. She bent over the counter, watching me as she took my order.

I did not even glance at her. She laughed, "Mister, you look like you been running all night."

"Yes. I been driving a long time."

She brought coffee, and I had two cups, black. The warm smell of food attacked me. I was having trouble keeping the black coffee down; I knew better than to try to eat.

The door behind me opened. A uniformed patrolman entered. I held my breath.

He looked along the counter, smiled at the waitress.
"Who owns the gray Studebaker out there?" He waited. I
did not speak because I could not. "Indiana license," he
added.

"That's mine." My voice croaked.

"You left your lights burning. You won't have any
battery."

"Oh? Thanks." I felt my shoulders sag. "I was just going."

The waitress laughed. "Don't mind him, Jay. He's trying
to set an endurance driving record of some kind."

My fists knotted; the last thing I wanted was to attract
attention of any kind. The cop was staring at me. I wanted
to yell. I had been so careful, getting on a north-south highway even before I stopped for gas. Now I pulled into a
drive-in on the road west and everybody in the place was
looking at me.

"You better pull into a motel somewhere and get some
sleep, mister," the cop said. "You look like you need it."

"Yes," I said. "I am tired." I dropped some money on the
counter and got out.

Just before dawn, I stopped beside a creek. I washed my
face, then filled the gas tank from the red can. I figured the
mileage. I was getting better than twenty-eight miles a gal-
lon. I opened the hood. The water was cool and had not
gone down even half an inch. It had not used any oil,
either.

Very careful driver, I thought bitterly as I threw the
empty gas can into the creek and stood watching it float
away.

By daylight I was on the Kansas prairies. There were no
trees except in the dry creek beds or in the carefully planted
wind breaks beside farm houses. The plains lay flat and yel-
low all the way to the horizon.

I drove all day, now at less than thirty miles an hour,
because as tired as I was, I was afraid to trust myself at any
higher speed.

I went through towns without seeing them. The plains
remained flat, there were small oil pumps in straight lines,
and grain elevators visible from twenty miles. At dusk I
drove through a small town named Oakley, a red brick

street, two drugstores, a garage, a hotel, and a railroad station.

I parked on a side street, the only car parked in the block. I rolled up the windows, locked the doors, and walked back to the hotel. I inquired about buses. The next bus going west to Denver passed through at nine that night. I thanked the woman and returned to the car.

Six miles west of town on highway forty, I pulled off the road into an unfenced wheat field. I made no attempt to conceal the car more than the darkness concealed it.

I stopped, cut the engine, sat in the silence for a moment. Cars passed infrequently on the highway, their headlights small. At last, I got the strength to move. I wiped the car as clean as I could of fingerprints, consciously remembering every place I had touched it, even the hood and water cap. I knew that fingerprints were useless unless made on a flat, smooth surface.

I left the key in the ignition. I bent under the dashboard and using the screwdriver cracked two of the tubes in the radio.

I walked around the car, checking everything. Finally satisfied, I lifted Cora, finding her rigid and awkward. I placed her on the front seat, under the steering wheel and let her topple over.

Good-by, Cora. This time it's really good-by.

I slammed the car door and walked toward Oakley. The stubbled wheatfields were dry, hard packed. I didn't even leave a footprint for them to trace.

I jogged along, every step seeming to vibrate against the top of my head. I stayed in the fields, walked around the town, came in across the railroad tracks and from the east.

At the bus station, I cleaned up as much as possible. I had a two-day growth of beard. I put on my glasses and couldn't even recognize myself.

I bought a ticket west to Denver and sat down to wait. I fought to stay awake. The bus was fifteen minutes late. I got on the bus, found a seat and stumbled into it. I fell asleep almost at once and didn't hear anything else until the bus pulled into the station at Denver.

I walked along, feeling better in the chilled air. Finally I stopped in a barber shop, got a shave, haircut, shine and manicure.

From the barber shop, I went to an air-conditioned restaurant. I ordered eggs and bacon, but when they were brought, I couldn't eat. The knot was still in my stomach.

In an exclusive men's shop, I bought underthings, a shirt and a gray suit. I had them wrap up my old clothes and in a cab, I removed the tailor's label from my old jacket.

There were dry-cleaners' symbols on my trouser pocket linings, but I didn't think they'd mean anything here in Denver. In the taxi I rode to the local Salvation Army. I handed them the bundle of clothes. I thought I carried it off well. "My wife says if I don't get rid of this old suit, she'll get rid of me." I smiled as I said it.

It was getting easier. Better. I was beginning to think about Laura, wanting her. I told myself the knot in my solar plexus was dissolving. I could not eat yet, but it would improve.

At the airport, I bought a ticket to Chicago. When the TWA clerk asked my name, I gave him a bland smile. What the hell, I thought. "Judge Richard Smith," I told him.

On the plane, I slept a little while, but it was not a deep sleep. I was restless, woke suddenly.

At Midway, I went to the Eastern Airlines desk and ordered a ticket to Tampa, feeling excitement building in me. I was going to be all right. As soon as I saw Laura again, I would be all right.

When the airlines clerk wanted my name, I paused. Then I gave them Gulick Williams' name.

We'd been in the air about an hour and I dozed. I came awake abruptly, white and shaken, sure I'd yelled. Trembling, I looked around. Nobody was paying any attention. I sank back, breathing through my mouth.

I couldn't escape the dream; I'd been sure Cora was sitting here beside me, rigid in rigor mortis, stretched out so I was crowded against the bulkhead.

I stayed awake until we landed in Tampa. I bought a newspaper. Of course there was no mention of Cora's body having been found. How many Western crimes ever get newspaper space in the east? How many times is the finding of a woman's body of wire service interest when the woman may have been driving alone and died of natural causes?

You might think the whole plan sounds screwy and complicated. Full of unnecessary risk. You might say a lawyer with ten years practice ought to be smarter. But that was my angle. Sometimes you can be too smart, you can outsmart yourself. And as I'd told Laura, I wanted nothing to do with courts, insurance companies, or even with the police. You could never be sure of anything with twelve good men and true. I wanted no more risk. I had gambled all at once on that drive west and I figured that car sitting out on the Kansas plains was going to give the cops and the FBI hemorrhages—a woman without identity, a car that belonged nowhere, dirt and road-film from half-a-dozen states. They'd be running around in circles, talking to themselves, but I gambled that the circle would never widen to include Summit, over a thousand miles east, or that they'd ever talk loud enough so the police in my community would overhear them. Sure, it was a complicated gimmick I was attempting, but if it kept me out of law courts, away from the cops and the hint of suspicion, that was what I wanted. When they tried to trace those clothes, that license plate, or the stolen car, or even Cora herself—I was going to get away with murder.

All I wanted now was to get to Laura.

I called her as soon as I reached Passagrille Beach. I chose a new motel. My heart lurched when I heard her voice.

"I've got to see you," I said.

"Yes."

"As soon as it's dark, Laura. I need you. Come over here."

"Yes. That will be better. I've been here so long now they call me a native."

"As soon as it's dark."

"Yes . . ." There was a long, charged silence. "Charley?"

"Yes?"

"Charley . . . did you do it?"

"Yes." My head was throbbing.

She did not answer. I heard her breathing, fast and deep above the hum of the wires. At last she replaced the receiver, very gently, and the connection was broken.

"It's done, Laura. That's all that matters. I don't want to talk about it. All I wanted was to get here to you so I wouldn't have to think about it."

She stirred on the bed, her eyes wide in the gray darkness. "Was it so bad, Charley?"

My head throbbed, the peace I'd hoped to find in her arms eluded me still. I exhaled heavily, rubbed my temples.

I could not keep it in any more. Talk spilled out, the bitterness underlining every word. I felt vile and I knew I'd never get the vileness out of me. I told her how it was, how sick I'd been after I knew Cora was dead, the living hell of driving over a thousand miles west with her body on the back seat.

She moved closer; her breath was hot against my face.

I felt her body, and her hands, and her lips, and it should have been like nothing on earth ever before. But it was as if I had been hungry too long, and now I had no taste for anything. There was nothing good. The more I tried to respond to her, the worse it became.

My head throbbed so terribly I thought my eyes would burst. . . .

We had meals served in the motel room. We didn't leave that room all day. I could forget everything, because I had what I wanted with Laura. The agony was that I could not have her, even yet.

"We must be careful, Laura."

"I don't want to be careful. We can be together now, Charley."

"No. Not until that divorce is final."

She pressed her mouth against mine, soft and warm, her breath fragrant and pleasant on my face. "It's over now, Charley. It's over. She's dead, and it's over."

I stood up, not because I wanted to, but because I was afraid I'd begin to believe her. "Not until I'm sure I'm not suspected."

She leaned forward on the bed, watching me, her green eyes gleaming. "Will you ever know that, Charley?"

Her voice made me shiver. All my own doubts were in it.

From my pocket, I took a letter Cora had written. I gave it to Laura.

"I want you to imitate Cora's handwriting, Laura. As closely as possible. You must write a letter back home to Cora's best friend. Tell her that you—Cora—and I have fought, and that you are getting a Florida divorce. Tell her you plan to leave Florida and go to South America after the decree is final—that you want to get away where you can forget."

"Will my handwriting fool Laura's best friend?"

"Maybe she hasn't seen too much of it. Anyway, you're upset. Don't be careful with it, scrawl your letters as though you're emotionally distraught. I don't care how you get it done, just so Edie receives this letter."

Laura reached out for me. "Charley, I don't want you to leave me. I'm afraid when you're gone."

I pressed my fists against my aching temples. "So am I," I said. "But it's going to end, Laura, and we'll have each other."

She sprang from the bed, pressed herself into my arms. She moved her mouth on mine and I felt better, as if maybe it was worth it. I was all right as long as Laura was close against me. I was complete.

Before I caught the train north, I bought the Denver newspapers. I heard the redhaired proprietor making a joke about my having to read about who had babies back home, but my head was throbbing and I couldn't answer him.

"Man, you're homesick," he said as I walked quickly away.

On the train I read the papers although my eyes seemed to bulge with the pain behind them.

I found it. At first the Kansas state police had thought the woman found in the car had died of a heart attack, but doctors said no, that she had suffocated. This puzzled the police, who advanced the theory she may have died from gas fumes before she could get the engine off. Because the car had an Indiana tag, a picture of the dead woman had been made. Foul play was suspected, and the FBI had been called in.

I read until I couldn't read any more. I could see the fit they were having—a license tag that didn't belong to the car; a car that belonged to nobody; Cora's fingerprints useless because they were on file nowhere.

I wadded up the papers, dropped them on the floor.

I took four aspirin, but my headache stayed right with me.

When the train pulled into Summit, I went first to the public pay station and called Victoria Haines.

"Cora has left me," I told her.

"I'm bleeding."

"I didn't expect you'd care, Victoria. I just thought you'd want to know."

She laughed. "Oh, you do want that judgeship, don't you, Charley?"

"I'm sorry I called you."

"Wait a minute, Charley. Sorry I needled you. But I can tell you, there's been no appointment made yet. Don't you want me to come down and pick you up?"

"We've got to be careful."

"Oh, Charley. Not that careful. You wait on the corner."

I wanted to yell at her. I didn't see how I could endure being in the same room with Victoria. My head throbbed.

What could I say? I wanted that judgeship. It was the most important thing left to me now.

"All right, Victoria," I said. . . .

I had six more aspirins at Victoria's apartment. She stroked my face until I had to touch it to be sure she hadn't worn a groove in it.

"I've missed you so terribly, Charley. The world was empty when you were gone."

The sweet smell of the room was torment. My throat ached. I knew how Cora had felt with that pillow choking out her life. . . .

I made a big thing of getting out of the taxi in front of my house on Forest Drive.

I timed it so that Myers was leaving for his office and Edie was with him as he walked out to the car.

She came around the hedge and met me on the walk in front of the house. Her face was worried. "Charley, what's the matter? Where's Cora?"

It wasn't hard to look distraught the way my head was aching.

"I may as well tell you, Edie. You know Cora and I hadn't been getting along for months—"

"It was your fault, Charley. Oh, I never knew anyone as crazy about her husband as Cora was."

"Well, she left me, anyhow."

"Charley. I don't believe it."

"It's true. It just didn't work out. We argued. When she left me, she said she was going to Miami. Well, I have this case coming up in court. I had to get back home. I couldn't run after her. Maybe she'll come to her senses."

Edie's face was gray. "You have sense, Charley. Get this silly case postponed and you'll fly down there and bring Cora home."

"I couldn't do that."

"Why not?"

"I went on this trip with her—when I couldn't afford the time. I did everything I could."

Her head tilted. "I don't think so, Charley. You just rushed her out of the house in the middle of the night. She didn't even get to buy any of the things she wanted to take."

"I did the best I could." The whole street was spinning, and my eyes felt as though they were going to fall out.

"No. You didn't." She turned away, her back rigid. "I don't think you ever really tried, Charley. Not ever."

A week later I got a notice from the lawyer Laura had hired in Florida. Cora was suing me for divorce, charging mental cruelty.

The morning paper carried a small item about it.

LOCAL ATTORNEY SUED

Charles Brower, well-known attorney and young social leader in Summit, and his wife, Cora Farland Brower, have separated. Mrs. Brower, prominent in local affairs, filed suit for divorce in Florida, charging mental cruelty. The couple has been married eleven years. There are no children.

I wrote the lawyer advising him that I would not be in Florida, and did not intend to contest the divorce. . . .

I did not know precisely what to do about the house. Clearly it belonged to Cora and would be demanded for her in the bill of divorce settlement. I didn't want to stay in it. I hated its stillness. I couldn't walk into the room where Cora had died. The housekeeper made up the bed and I closed the door and left it closed.

I was standing out on the sunporch when Edie Myers came through the hedge at the place she and Cora had hacked out to make visiting back and forth easier.

When she came through the door I saw she had a letter in her hand. I felt the increase of tension. This was the letter I'd told Laura to write from Florida. A lot would depend on how Edie Myers fell for that letter.

Her face was stiff. She made no effort to conceal her dislike for me. "I have a letter from Florida . . ." She paused. My heart speeded and then slowed. I felt the blood seep down from my face. "It's from Cora."

"Oh?" I started out across the yard, pretending it didn't matter, yet afraid to let her see my face.

"Yes. It's a strange letter, Charley. Doesn't sound like Cora."

"What does Cora sound like?"

"Are you so bitter, Charley? If there's any divorce, it's your fault. All your fault."

"We Indians have an old saying, Edie. Walk a mile in my moccasins before you find fault with me."

"Oh, I don't say Cora was perfect. But she loved you. She would have done anything to keep her home with you."

"Maybe she was finally convinced, Edie, that it was no good."

"I didn't come over here to argue with you. I have nothing to say to you, Charley. I've said all I have to say. If Cora is in Florida—"

"Didn't you get a letter from her from down there?"

"—you better fly down there and get her back. I would not have come over here at all, but I wanted to see something that Cora wrote."

I jerked my head around. "Why?"

She had socked that one to me hard. I knew what was coming next. I held on tightly. And it came.

"I want to compare her writing with this letter. It seems so odd, not like Cora."

"For God's sake, what's the matter with you?"

"Nothing. Isn't there a letter around here from Cora, something she wrote?"

"Not that I know of, off hand."

"Hasn't she written to you?"

"Why should she?"

She stared at me for a long time. At last she shook her head. "I wish I could find something—this writing is all wrong."

"Maybe Cora was upset. What do you want, Edie? What are you trying to say?"

She shrugged. "I don't know—"

"If you think something is wrong, tell me."

"It's nothing, Charley." She backed away to the door. "It's just that everything is so strange. Cora letting you drag her away from here not taking any of the things she planned to take. Then deciding to get a divorce when she's told me a hundred times she would never get a divorce. And this letter that doesn't even sound like her, and saying she's going to South America—"

"Oh?"

"Didn't you know? Does that sound like Cora? She dreaded being among strangers, and now she says she wants to go to South America to forget. It seems to me that if Cora was unhappy she'd want to be with all her friends so they could help her."

I stared at her. "Maybe she finally figures her friends have helped her too much now—running to her with every lie they could think up."

She laughed. She pushed the door open. "Don't sound wounded, Charley. It's all out of character. The dashing young lawyer, too damned good for little Cora. And now you don't even care that she's going off to South America all by herself, when she was afraid to go downtown alone."

She walked away across the yard, the letter still gripped in her fist. I stood there cursing her under my breath.

That evening I was in the front room. I had almost convinced myself that it would not look strange for me to close this house and go to a hotel. One thing, I'd be away from Edie Myers and her sixth sense. Funny she should have such a highly developed sixth sense when all the first five were so poor.

The doorbell rang. I glanced at the windows, saw it was dark. I was afraid it was Victoria Haines. Things had been very quiet for the past two days.

It was Frank Vanness.

I knew in that moment what the rest of my life was going to be. It didn't make any difference if I were suspected, or if I got away with it completely. That was what made it unbearable. I'd never know when that knock would come, and some man would be standing there, the man with all the answers.

"May I come in, Counsellor?"

"Sure. Why not?" I stepped aside, leaning slightly against the door jamb. He walked past me.

"I won't beat around the bush with you, Counsellor." He twirled his hat in his hand, looked around the room. "I read in the paper about you and the wife getting a divorce. Read that she was in Florida. So we don't take this thing very seriously."

I swallowed hard, offered him a drink, watched him shake his head. "What thing?"

"It's for you, just as much as against you, Counsellor. You can see that."

"Whatever you say. Sure you won't have a drink?"

"Not this time. Rack me up a rain check, Counsellor."

"You mean I'll have to see you again?" I tried to laugh. So did he. "Might. Who knows?"

14

Laura was back in the office next morning. I could not wait to get there to see her. I'd known she was flying in at night, but I didn't dare go near the airport; I sat by the phone, but didn't dare call her.

I had promised myself I had taken care of all the angles, but suddenly I dreaded and feared gossip. The divorce was not going to help me get Gulick Williams' job. I'd have to do everything I could to balance that strike against me. I was afraid to be seen chasing my secretary, or even displaying an interest in her.

She was in the reception room. I should grab her in my arms, welcome her home. She was in this, all the way, accessory after the fact. But I was on guard even against my deepest emotions.

Laura was too excited to notice my preoccupation. She locked the outer door when I entered. Finally, she pulled away from me, and I saw the agony in her eyes. "We must talk, Charley."

"We've got to be careful, too. That divorce isn't final."

"Why do we wait, Charley? Why don't we just run away? Tell people you're going to Europe. You've that much money. I'll meet you there. We'll wait until the divorce is final. We'd never have to come back."

Her eyes were hollow and encircled. She seemed to have lost weight.

"What's the matter, Laura?"

"Nothing, Charley. It's just we're taking chances we don't have to take. We can get out of the country now. Go somewhere where there is no extradition."

"I don't want such a place. I want that half-million. I want to get away with this."

Her mouth trembled. "But if you can't?"

"I can. I'm going to stay here. It may be rough. I've got to win. There's a chance I might get on the Circuit Court bench—"

"Charley—you wouldn't take it?"

"Why wouldn't I? I'm going to take it. I'll sweat it out." I tried to laugh. "We've got these few minutes anyhow. Come here, baby."

I pulled her into my arms.

It seemed almost at once she was gone again and I was alone. I paced my office. If I sat down, I could not concentrate and started pacing again.

For a little while, when she was with me, it was all right. Then she'd gotten the notice forwarded from her motel: it was time to appear for her hearing before a judge. The time she'd been with me had raced, the way a rollercoaster does on a long downgrade. When Laura got the notice, she was more tense than ever, began talking again about running, finding a country from which we'd never be extradited. I was on edge too. I told her I was going to be Judge Charles R. Brower. Nothing was going to stop me.

She cried for a long time before she left. I told her if I'd been going to capitulate to her fears, I'd have given in to my own long ago.

I poured myself another drink. I had killed off almost a fifth of bourbon, but it was like drinking water. I couldn't get it off my mind that there should be some way to speed it up, get it over with. That was the worst of it, not knowing what they were doing about Cora and the stolen Studebaker out in Kansas. I wanted it to end, just so I could get an hour of sleep. I wanted to know what kind of investigation the Governor's office was making of me, what they were finding out. I told myself I had a good record, that I had nothing to worry about. There was nothing to do but wait.

The phone rang. I knew who was calling and I didn't want to answer it. Victoria Haines. When I thought about her now, I felt stifled by enveloping perfumes. She had an insatiable hunger, and she had me right where she wanted me.

If I wasn't nice to her, if I didn't play along, she could say the wrong things to the Governor, and I'd never get that judgeship. Suddenly it seemed I had killed for that job, and I had to have it, no matter what I had to do for Victoria Haines. Once I got that job I could drop her, and there was nothing she could do.

I picked up the receiver. It was Victoria, all right. The sixth time she'd called that day.

"Charley, you must give me an answer. I've told you. I've reserved a suite at Barrington Springs for the weekend. I'm not going up there and wait for you. Either you are going to meet me there, or I'm going to cancel the reservation." Her voice dropped, chilled. "I don't think you want me to cancel it, Charley."

"I told you I couldn't get away just now, Victoria. No matter how much I'd like to, I just can't do it."

"I think you can. Nothing is more important right now than getting to see you. After all, Charley, you started this, you know. You wanted me—you ran after me—"

"I still want you, Victoria."

"Whether you do or not, I think I know what you do want. I think you're smart enough to know I haven't the mildest temper in the world."

"Victoria, you know—"

"Stop stalling, Charley."

"All right. All right." I didn't give a damn if the helplessness showed in my tone. She wouldn't care about that. "I'll meet you there."

"Saturday, Charley."

I left the office Saturday at noon. I carried the small suitcase that had become almost part of my uniform since I'd gotten involved with Victoria Haines, the hungry tigress.

"Counsellor."

I was on the curb awaiting a cab when Mike Welch pulled up in front of me in a new Cad. I had the unexplained feeling he'd been waiting down here for me to come out of the building. I tried to tell myself that didn't make sense, but I had not been able to forget that stolen Studebaker.

"Where you going. Counsellor?"

"Got to make a train," I said.

"Get in. Run you to the station. Glad to do you a favor."

I got in. I stared straight ahead. He drove like a wild man. "Thought we were quits on the favors, Mike."

"Little favors. Man likes to do little favors he don't expect nothing out of. Right, Counsellor?"

"If you say so, Mike."

He slipped through after a light showed red. He stepped hard on the gas, then suddenly released the pedal.

"Say, Counsellor, you ever get in touch with that hot-car boy?"

"Which one?"

"Oh, come on, Counsellor. The one you fought thirty minutes with me to get name and personal phone number. That one."

"No," I said. "I changed my mind. Why?"

He chewed on his cigar. "No reason. Good thing though you never called him. FBI found a car, traced it to a town up in Michigan. What you think of that, Counsellor? Pretty smart, those boys. Huh?"

My fists clenched tight. "What kind of car?"

He glanced at me a moment, looked back at the street just in time to swerve around a storage truck.

"Who knows? Who cares? It don't touch us. Dead body in that car. Craziest thing, they came on to my friend. They got rough with him. Really worked him over."

I sat there, waiting. There had to be more. But I couldn't ask. Mike Welch's face was taut, waiting for me to show any interest.

"Glad you never used that name and number, Counsellor. Because me? I sure would hate to have that boy mad at me after he had a round with them Feds."

He swerved the car into the curb in front of the station.

"This is it, Counsellor. Have yourself a ball."

I got out. Mike Welch stared at me a moment, stepped on the gas. This was it. He knew a lot of things I had to know, and he wasn't going to tell me. This had to end, because now it was just a race to see whether I or my perfect murder came unglued first.

I was shaking as though I had a chill by the time I got off the train at the Barrington Springs station. I stared at the Barrington Springs Hotel station wagon, and at the other cars parked beside it. I thought how crazy it was. Once I had wanted people to see me when I was with Victoria Haines; now I got ill at the thought somebody might spot us together.

"Charley. Charley-sweet. Over here."

Victoria was in a hired car. I forced myself to grin and walked over. Other weekend guests piled into the station wagon and the other cars. Victoria gave me a juicy kiss, clinging to me. Even after she moved away, the strong odor of her make-up remained in my nostrils.

We drove to the hotel. She told me I didn't have to check in, she had done that for me. When a bellhop tried to take my bag, she tossed him a half-buck tip and told him I was a big strong boy. I could carry my own bag.

I tried to stall her into the lobby lounge for a drink, but she wasn't buying any of that, either. She had everything up in our rooms. This girl had thought of everything.

When we were up there, and the cloying scent was already beginning to suffocate me, she pressed against my back, put her arms around me and squashed me against her. I felt a sudden revulsion that made me almost physically ill.

"Isn't this perfect?" she said.

"Sure." I was wishing I knew what those FBI men were doing out in Kansas.

She pressed against me harder, her body giving. "Being alone in a hotel room with a man does crazy things to me, Charley. I could hardly wait for you to get here."

What was wrong with the bellhops? I thought.

She was crowding me. I could hardly breathe even with the windows open and the breezes pouring in.

"I thought you were mad at me."

"Not now. Not when you're here with me, Charley."

She was working on her clothes. I lay back, closed my eyes so I would not have to see her when she spilled from her bra and her girdle. Maybe if I didn't look at her . . .

"You sure don't act as if you want me very bad," she said.

One of the worst tortures yet devised for man is having to pretend ardor for a woman he despises.

"I'm here," I said. "Isn't that enough?"

"It's something," she said. "But not enough."

We didn't leave the rooms that weekend. She ordered our meals sent up; wouldn't even let me handle that little chore. She smiled and stroked me all the time, and kept telling me she wanted to do everything for me, she didn't want me to move except to love her. And that's just about the way it was.

My mouth felt raw when she covered it with her full lips. She ran her hands over me until it was like crawling ants. The cloying scent never receded for a moment. I had cabin fever the way no man ever contracted it before. And all that time, mixed up with her perfume and her hands and her mouth was the agony over what the police were doing.

She wouldn't let me sleep. I suppose I could not have slept, anyway, but if only I could get away from her just long enough to stand at the window and get a breath of fresh air. It didn't happen that way. She talked about how beautiful I was going to look as a judge, the things we were going to do when my divorce was final and we no longer had to hide like this.

I had to get out of there.

I thought it never would, but Monday came. I talked Victoria out of accompanying me back to Summit on the train. I told her unless she had positive knowledge I wasn't going to get that judge appointment, we had to make a pretense at respectability.

I got out of there before dawn and caught the milk train back to town. I couldn't breathe deeply enough; I couldn't get enough water to drink.

I was still thirsty, when I reached my office. All I was thinking about was getting at the water cooler.

Frank Vanness was waiting for me at my door. . . .

"Been away, Counsellor?" He eyed the suitcase, looking me over as I unlocked the door and told him to come in.

My mind was whirling. I was too depleted, too thirsty to think clearly. I was sure that something had broken in Cora's murder. Something I had overlooked, something I had forgotten. Rapidly, I checked over everything, but couldn't see where I had gone wrong. I didn't look at Vanness. I couldn't trust myself to let him see the fear that must be showing in my eyes.

I walked straight to the water cooler.

I ran a glass of water, feeling the glass chill against my fingers.

"Been doing some heavy drinking, Counsellor?"

"Why?" I spoke over my shoulder.

"Heavy drinking, and need a lot of cold water the next morning."

"No," I said. "It's just that I've been away. Nothing tastes so good as hometown water when you've been away, Frank. You ever notice that?"

He watched me drink. "Where you been?"

I had no idea what he was leading up to, how much he knew, or why he was waiting for me.

"Just a little business trip," I said.

"Yeah. But do you mind saying where?"

I still wanted that judgeship. I wasn't going to jeopardize it until I found out what was on his mind.

"Chicago," I said. "I flew up."

His brow tilted. But after a moment he shrugged. He leaned against a desk, watching me. His voice was low, "I guess you haven't heard, then."

"No. Heard what?"

"Your wife."

Somebody had slapped the world from under me. I wanted to sit down before I fell.

I whispered it at him. "Cora?"

"You look bad, Counsellor. Why don't you sit down?" That soft voice hadn't changed. This didn't go with his jut-jawed coldness.

I sat down on the reception room couch. All right, Vanness, I thought, let's get it over with. "What about Cora?"

"She's been murdered, Mr. Brower. I hate to be the one to tell you. We just got word. It was brutal."

Brutal? My head jerked up. "Cora?"

"Yes, sir. We just got the word from the cops down there in Florida. Somebody beat her to death."

I looked at him a moment, and he began to sail slowly, moving in a gray arc before my head. I opened my mouth, tried to speak. But there were no words, and I crumpled forward on the floor, passed out cold.

15

I came out of it slowly, the reluctance to start living again the strongest thing in me. Vanness kept waving smelling salts under my nose until I sat up and moved away from it.

"Take it easy, Mr. Brower."

Take it easy. Laura was dead. Laura. Somebody had killed Laura. Beaten to death.

I covered my head with my hands. It didn't make sense. It wheeled around in my brain and didn't make sense at all. Sure, Vanness said Cora. The cops wired from Florida that it was Cora. Why not? Wasn't Laura registered down there as Mrs. Charley Brower? Vanness showed me the Summit paper, and they had printed Cora's picture with the wire service story from Florida. That morning in a motel room, Mrs. Cora Brower, brutally slain, police seeking unknown assailant.

I hunched there reading the story, the phony local parts, Cora's birth, marriage, clubs, all the morgue stuff the paper had printed when they couldn't get in touch with me.

I kept swallowing the sickness that gorged up in my throat. I thought about Gulick Williams' judgeship, and I knew it was gone. But that didn't seem very important. The police had only the first installment of this story, and it was all cockeyed. Wait until they started to dig. Wait until they found out that wasn't Cora at all, that it was Laura Meadill posing as Cora, getting a divorce from me in Cora's name.

I shuddered, refusing to think any further.

"Mr. Brower?"

I was shaking. I looked up. I was startled to see pity in Frank Vanness' blue eyes. I looked away quickly.

"Why don't you let me take you home, Mr. Brower? Nothing we can do around here."

"Sure. Come on. Let's go." I glanced at the wilted rose in the vase on Laura's desk. I shivered. Laura was dead. Down in Florida, Laura was dead. I remembered suddenly that she had seemed nervous and upset while she was here in Summit. She had wanted me to take her away, out of the country, kept talking about going before it was too late.

Well, it was really too late now.

We drove through town in Vanness' police cruiser. It was battered inside; the seats were torn and there was blood or something splattered along the inside door facing. I tried to look at the town, the buildings and trees and people as we passed, but they had no reality.

"Florida police want you to come down there."

"No!" The word burst out of me.

He glanced at me, scowling. "They need you, Mr. Brower. It's murder. One thing, they'll expect you to identify the body."

I didn't speak.

"Another thing they'll expect you to cooperate on, is who might have hated your wife enough to kill her like that."

"I don't know."

"You think about it, Mr. Brower. This is a bad crime. I know you and the wife were not hitting it off so well, and she was down there getting a divorce. But this is a lot worse than divorce. This is a killing, and the police are going to need your help to find that killer."

"I don't know what I could tell them."

"We can talk it over."

"We?"

"Yeah. Police want me to fly down there with you. I told them—well, I said you were a friend of mine, and I'd be glad to go along with you. I want to help you, Mr. Brower. I know we've seen eye to toe on a lot of things, but when a man's in trouble like this—"

I swallowed back the sickness, thinking, If you only knew.

"There's one thing, though," he said. His voice had a regretful tone as though he disliked bringing it up just now.

"Yeah?"

"That trip you took."

I swallowed back the sickness again. It was more difficult.

"Yes."

"Chicago."

I didn't answer. He glanced at me. "You say you flew? I hope there was somebody that you know that might've seen you."

"What are you talking about?" I knew what he was talking about, all right.

"I hate to say it Mr. Brower. But I might as well. Them Florida police will certainly say it. You might as well be ready for them. Now on this flight to Chicago. You see anybody you knew? A man could fly from here to Florida and back over Sunday, Mr. Brower. Them Florida police are sure going to think that. So if there's somebody that can say you were really in Chicago, you better get in touch with them right away."

We moved through the streets for what seemed a long time without speaking. My mind was racing. I kept thinking I might as well give up. It was just a matter of time now. The trap had been sprung—and not from Kansas at all, but from Florida. There'd be no appointment to a judge's bench, there'd be none of Cora's money. I couldn't see what would be left. I felt as though something were crawling all over my body. All I could think was that maybe somehow I could save my skin.

I was down to that now.

"Well, Mr. Brower, how about it? You able to think of anybody?"

"I know somebody . . ."

"Yeah."

"This person—can swear I wasn't in Florida over the weekend."

"That's fine."

"But—I well, I lied to you, Frank."

I felt the chill start in that car.

"Yeah? What about?"

"About Chicago. I didn't exactly go to Chicago. I didn't fly."

"No? Where were you?"

"I was in Barrington Springs."

"The whole weekend?"

"That's right. From Saturday until early this morning."

"You got somebody can swear to that?"

"Yes . . . Victoria Haines."

That cut it. Whatever pity I had seen in his eyes was gone. His mouth was a tight line; he was a cop again, all cop, and I was on the other side of a high wall.

Vanness swung the battered cruiser into the driveway. There were three police cruisers there awaiting us.

First I suppose they were staked out to deliver the news of Cora's murder in Florida to me if I returned home instead of the office. Then I shook my head bitterly. That was not the reason they were there. That was too simple.

Two uniformed policemen leaped off the veranda strode out to meet us before we could get out of the cruiser.

That's the way with trouble. It can never hit you fast enough, or hard enough.

"Sergeant," one of the cops said to Vanness. "Been waiting for you, got some airmailed pictures here from down in Florida. Something's cockeyed."

This cop had glossy photos in his fist. I stared at them as if I could never pull my gaze away. But I didn't have to see them to know what they were. The way the sun hit them they still appeared wet from the developing solution, they were that new, but to me they were already old.

Vanness swung out of the car and reached for the photos.

The cop surrendered them and then they crowded each side of Vanness looking at them as if they'd never seen them before. They did not even remember me, but it did not matter. My legs were tired. I did not move. It felt fine just sitting there in that car.

Finally, Vanness turned and looked at me. His jaw had receded slightly and his squinted eyes were wide.

"Brower—"

I just looked at him.

"There's really something cockeyed. This woman isn't Mrs. Brower. She's dead, but she isn't Mrs. Brower at all."

I still didn't speak. I was too tired to pretend anything. I didn't have to reach for it any more. They were slugging me with everything already.

"I know this woman," Vanness said. His voice sounded strange. "It ain't Mrs. Brower. It sure ain't Mrs. Brower, and yet it is somebody I know—"

He stared at the pictures some more, shuffling them in his hands.

He swung around, jerked his head at me. "Here, Brower. Come take a look at these."

I pushed myself out of the car, walked woodenly around

the front end. One of the cops made a place for me beside Vanness. I glanced around, looking for something to lean against. There was nothing.

"Look at these pictures. Know this woman?"

They were the brutal, unblinking police lab pictures technicians take at the scene of the crime. They were not prettied up at all. Vanness held each one before my face for what seemed an interminable time. In an instant I saw more than I wanted to see, more than I could take. Laura, I thought. My God, poor Laura.

I was afraid I was going to be sick. Vanness bumped me with his shoulder. "How about it, Brower? What you got to say. Who is this woman?"

I wanted to speak. There was no sense holding out information like this from him now. The police at St. Petersburg probably already knew the truth. Laura had only registered as Mrs. Charles Brower. She had not carried the masquerade any further. It had not seemed necessary. There must have been personal belongings, or identification cards, marked with her real name. But it was hard to speak. It was taking one more step toward the electric chair.

I licked at my lips. There was a barrier in my throat, and the words had to clear it.

"Come on, Brower. Speak up. You know this woman—she lives here in Summit. She works around here. Why, I've seen her recently. Oh, yeah. Sure. Good Lord, Brower, this is your secretary."

I nodded. It wasn't easy.

"Laura. Laura something," Vanness said, scowling. He no longer expected anything from me.

"Then this ain't Mr. Brower's wife?" one of the cops said. "That's what they told us at headquarters. But they say she sure is registered at that motel as Mrs. Charles Brower, of Summit."

Vanness glanced at me. He spoke to one of the cops. "Take this guy up inside the house. Let him sit down before we have to carry him in there."

The cop touched my arm and I moved like an automoton. He waited while I unlocked the door. We entered the foyer. The emptiness in the house overwhelmed me.

"Sit down in there," the cop told me. He was a young

fellow, under thirty with a hectic flush and nervous hands. Vanness' voice had told him that I was not due any deference. Earlier, I'd been the bereaved husband. Now I might be the murderer. I stumbled into the front room and sank down in my reading chair.

The room spun oddly. I heard the front door slam, but I didn't even look up when Vanness crossed the room, snapped on the reading lamp beside my chair and tilted its shade so that the glare struck the side of my face.

"Look up," Vanness ordered.

I lifted my head. The light was painful in my eyes. I tried to lower them.

"You heard me, mister." Vanness' voice was sharp. "I got a question I want to ask you. A big one."

I stared up at him. I was groggy, too groggy to think about the rights I had always fought the police over with clients of mine. Right now I was no client. I was hanging on the ropes, reeling. I wasn't thinking. I was reduced to nothing.

"Now this secretary of yours. This Laura—"

"Meadill."

"Yeah. Laura Meadill. Now we got the word from the police down in Florida that this Meadill woman has been posing as your wife down there for almost three months. Part of that time she has been up here. I know. I've seen her in your office. She's dead. She's been murdered. But that's not what's troubling me. I want to know something else, Brower. I want a straight answer."

"Yeah?"

"Where's your wife, Brower? Where's Cora Brower?"

Vanness leaned over me. "You better know. The sheriff's office down there in Florida wants you, Brower. They want some explanations. We're going down there, but before we go we're straightening out the loose ends up here. You're trying to play somebody for a sucker, Brower. But it ain't going to be me."

"Don't know—what you're talking about."

"You don't have to know what I'm talking about. You're going to sit right there and I'm going to tell you what I'm talking about. I want you to hear it. It didn't mean much, without this murder, and these pictures. It didn't look good, but it didn't add up to anything. Just a guy with hot pants who's playing around with one of his wife's friends."

He stopped talking, his voice loud and cold in the silent house. The two uniformed patrolmen stood rigid, watching him.

"But now let's see what we got. We start with a call from a crank—a letter from some anonymous character. He says your wife is not in Florida. He says that something is wrong and we ought to check.

"So I check. You seemed convinced your wife was in Florida. Told me about the letter Mrs. Myers got. You want to hear about that letter? It was never wrote by your wife. No, sir. I got the testimony of a graphology expert on that. Sure, I agreed with you. Poor Mrs. Brower. All upset. Didn't care how she wrote.

"Then Mrs. Myers. She didn't think that letter came from your wife, either. Seems there was a lot of things your wife wanted to do before she left town, yet she left without doing any of them, without taking any of the things she planned to take.

"So maybe your wife was never in Florida at all. If she wasn't, what have we got? Looks like you and this Meadill were in on a murder—of your wife."

I sat forward. "You're crazy. It's Laura who's dead, not Cora."

"All right. So maybe Cora is not dead. Where is she, Brower?"

"I don't know."

"Where's your wife?"

"I told you. I don't know."

"And I'm telling you. You better find out. We got a dead woman down there in Florida. But we also got you just coming back from a weekend trip that you've lied about once—maybe twice."

"I told you how you could check that weekend."

"And don't think I won't check. But what does it give

us? Something else. Another motive for killing?"

"Why would I want to kill Laura Meadill?"

"I don't know yet. But I'll find out. And now you're feeling better. The smart lawyer."

"I'm smart enough to tell you to arrest me, or get off my back."

"Technically, mister, you are under arrest. Just let's don't get away from our theme. I didn't say that you wanted to kill Meadill. That will come later. I'm talking about why you would want to kill your wife."

"Who said my wife was dead?" The words were ripped out of me.

"You haven't said where she is."

"I've told you I don't know."

"So maybe she is dead."

"What are you driving at?"

"At you, mister. At a guy running around with the friend of his wife. And his wife? Brokenhearted. Enough so that friends will believe she is down in Florida getting a divorce."

"She said she was."

"Oh, come on down, Counsellor. You're smarter than that. There ain't but one Mrs. Charles Brower down there in Florida. And we got a picture of her. Dead. Laura Meadill posing as your wife. Dead down there in Florida. But that don't tell us where your wife is."

"All right, maybe she isn't in Florida."

"Sure. Maybe she ain't. But if she ain't down in Florida where is she?"

"I don't know."

"If she didn't write that letter saying she was down there in Florida—"

"Who says she didn't?"

"I say she didn't. Experts say she didn't write that letter. So what do we do on that? We show them that letter again—only this time we let them compare it with the handwriting of your secretary. How about that, Brower? What do you think we'll get then?"

"I don't know. This is your pipe dream."

"Yeah. You had your own dream, didn't you, playing fast and loose with this Victoria Haines. Why not? What did your wife have except a lot of money? How much, Brower? And if she died, who would get it?"

"Who said she died?"

"Nobody has told me anything about her. That's what I'm waiting for. Meantime, I'm telling you what it looks like to me. You hired this Laura Meadill to go to Florida and pose as your wife and get a Florida divorce. Had her write a phony letter, saying that when it was final, she wasn't coming home, this Cora wasn't. No, she was going to South America. All her friends tell me that she was afraid to make a train trip alone—wouldn't even ride in an elevator alone. But suddenly she is going to South America."

"She can go where she wants."

"Sure. But why South America? A woman like that? I don't think so. South America is just a good, far place, isn't it?"

I didn't answer. My eyes were watering from the glaring light.

"What happens when she gets down in South America? Your wife, I mean. Surely this Laura Meadill wasn't going to South America. But what happens. In a year or so you get a letter from your wife—your ex-wife Cora—and she tells you that she is going to marry some Latin señor."

I couldn't speak. Vanness had it as if he were reading from the mental script I had carefully prepared all these weeks, thinking I was clever, original and unbeatable. Sweat dropped along my ribs.

"Is that it, Brower? Is that the pattern?"

"I don't know what you're talking about. My secretary was killed in Florida. Now you're accusing me of killing not only her—but my wife too. I told you I can prove where I was last weekend."

"You're going to get a chance to do that."

"Then arrest me, or drop it."

"There's still that other little matter. Your wife. Wouldn't give you a divorce. Is that it, Brower? Loved you because you were such a dog? Loved you so much you had to kill her to get rid of her?"

I was sweating. "The woman who is dead," I whispered at him, my voice hoarse and choking, "is named Meadill. Meadill. Meadill."

"Sure it is. But what I want to know is, where is Cora Brower?"

The doorbell rang sharply and Vanness straightened, sighing.

"Bigley." He spoke over his shoulder. "See who that is at the door. Tell 'em we don't want any." His laugh was sharp. "That is unless he knows where Cora Brower is."

Bigley walked out of the room, and returned with two more patrolmen.

I stared at them blankly. I was too beaten now to care what news they brought.

"Vanness." They called Frank over and I sank back in the chair, pushed the light away.

I watched them talking, looking at a new set of pictures.

Finally, Vanness spun on his heel, strode back over to me. His face was cold, that jaw jutted.

"Down in Florida they know more about this Meadill woman than we do, Brower. But they don't know as much about you. As far as they know, you're a bereaved husband. They don't know about Victoria Haines and your wife's money—"

"No more than you do."

"I know plenty. Because they're looking for another man." He watched my face for the effect of that.

I stopped breathing. This didn't have to hit me as hard as it did. I must have realized somebody beat Laura to death in her motel room. The chances were that it was a man. But somehow, in the confusion, another man had not seemed real. A man who was intimate enough to be in her room early Sunday morning—the pictures showed what she was wearing. A man who hated—or loved—Laura enough to kill her in passion and anger.

Another man. A lover. Laura's lover. I had to say it over and over to believe it, even now.

My face must have told Vanness plenty because he laughed. It was a contemptuous sound. "What did I tell you, Counsellor? Years ago. If she'll step out *with* you— later, she'll step out *on* you. Every time, Counsellor."

"I don't know what you're talking about."

His voice was sharp. "This is what I'm talking about. Those people in the sheriff's office down there sent this

picture because they thought Mr. Brower might know the
man suspected of murdering Mrs. Brower. They don't
know yet it ain't Mrs. Brower. But they do send word that
her divorce there is almost final. Is that the divorce you sent
Laura Meadill down there to get, Brower?"

"I don't know what you're talking about."

He laughed. "So you flew down there Saturday, and
spent the night with her?"

Now I laughed, a forced sound. "They're looking for
another man, remember?"

"Sure they are. Because they don't know what we
know. They say the neighbors said this man was with her
all the time down there—and that he checked out suddenly Sunday morning and that he was using a phony
name. What phony name did you use down there,
Counsellor?

"I told you I wasn't in Florida."

"I heard you. You got everything to win; this guy has
nothing." He leaned forward, thrust a picture at me. I
stared at it. I stared for a long time because from the first
instant it seemed familiar—waved hair, penciled mustache,
twisted smile.

"You know him, Brower?" Vanness said. "Somebody
who was a friend of your secretary's?"

I shook my head.

"I never saw him before."

Then suddenly it came rushing over me, and I remembered this boy. Sure. Why not? It was the guy in the apartment across the patio from Laura. The oily one. When I
asked her about him, what had she said? What a quaint
expression? What an old-fashioned expression. Oh,
brother. Neat. Changing the subject without appearing to
be interested. Her boy friend. All the neighbors said they
were together all the time. The gigolo. I saw the way he had
stood there, saying he needed a cigarette, keeping me
speared in that light from his room while he looked me
over, staring at me with that twisted smile on his face.

Suddenly that smile had a new meaning. It meant he
knew me. He knew Laura, and he knew all about me.
That's what that smile had been saying.

Only I had been too busy to listen.

How could I tell Vanness that I had seen this man just
once, and that was in Florida in front of Laura
Meadill's apartment. All I could do was think about Laura's
begging me to leave the country, begging me to leave with
her while we still had a chance. Twice now, I'd just missed.
The night I killed Cora—the telephone rang and I could
have had Gulick Williams' spot on the circuit court bench.
But it was just too late. An hour before, that telephone call
might have changed everything. And then Laura had
begged me to get out of the country—afraid to tell me about
that man in Florida.

Vanness leaned over me. "Listen to me. I want to know
where your wife is."

"Find her then."

"I'll find her. Meantime, if I had my way, I'd jail you on
just what I know."

"What you think you know is not good enough, Vanness."

"Feel chipper now, Counsellor? Oh, boy. The way you
looked in your office when I told you your wife had been
killed down there in Florida. You looked so sick I was sorry
for you. Sorry for you! And all the time I was thinking how
you were hit by the news of your wife's death, it wasn't
that at all. You knew it wasn't your wife. You knew your
wife wasn't even in Florida. When I said Florida, you knew
it was your secretary who was dead—and I was fitting you
for a place in the electric chair."

"If I'd known she was dead, I wouldn't have been
shocked."

"There are answers. And I'll have them. I'll have them
all. When I got them, we can start shaving your head."

"You're a real comic."

"No. I'm no comic at all. I know that, Counsellor. I'm just
a boy does his job. I hate killers. Especially the kind that
think they're clever and then come up with something like
that South America gimmick."

The doorbell rang as Vanness turned to walk away. He glanced over his shoulder. "Looks like another load of bad news for you."

I stood up.

Bigley opened the front door, and I recognized Victoria Haines' sugary tones.

I trembled. Vanness had turned now and was laughing at me, his eyes cold and deadly.

Victoria walked into the room. I stared at her, wondering how she could be such a fool. Hadn't she seen all those police cars out front? Did she need an engraved invitation to get lost at a time like this? Didn't she have sense enough to know that people had linked our names, and that she was helping me to the electric chair?

Vanness didn't look at Victoria. He didn't take his gaze from my face.

"Charley. Poor Charley." She held out her arms and ran to me, ignoring the cops. Over her head, I saw the knowing glances. "I came as quickly as I could, Charley. As soon as I heard. Poor Cora—murdered like that!"

I tried to hold her away.

"Victoria, there's something you ought to know—"

"Who could have done such a thing? Who, Charley? Such a brutal thing. Poor Cora!"

Frank Vanness, laughed. It was an ugly, brutal sound in the silent room.

Victoria stepped back slightly. She stared at Frank Vanness. Her face was white.

"There's just a slight error, Mrs. Haines—"

"How do you know my name?"

"I'm afraid there's quite a lot I know about you."

She frowned, her face still white, and then she turned and looked at me.

Why the hell didn't you stay home, I thought.

"Charley, what is it? What's the matter?"

Frank Vanness laughed again. "It's just that you're mixed up, Victoria. It wasn't his wife that was killed. At least not the one you read about in the papers. By the way, you just get back in town?"

Her head tilted. She ignored his last question. "But Cora's picture was in the morning paper. I saw it."

"Yeah. But it was a mistake. It was not Brower's wife that got herself killed Sunday morning. It was his secretary. Laura Meadill. You know her?"

Victoria's face went white. It was as if he had struck her. I felt weak and leaned against the arm of the chair. Victoria did know Laura Meadill. That was clear enough in her shocked expression.

Vanness stepped toward her before she recovered. "There's a question I'd like to ask you, Victoria."

"My name is Mrs. Haines."

"Is it? When I meet your kind of woman, I never call them anything but first names."

"Why, you're insulting!"

"I call them as I see them, Victoria. You want trouble with me, why you go right ahead. You start it."

She stared at him for a moment with narrowed blue eyes and jutting jaw. Her gaze wavered, her mouth trembled and she turned, looking at me.

I didn't meet her eyes at all.

"You ready to answer my question, Victoria?"

"I don't have to answer your questions."

"You will sooner or later. And it concerns your boy friend here."

Her head jerked up at that word. She stood tense, waiting.

"It will be a big help to Brower, Victoria, if you cooperate. He says he was with you over the weekend. Would you care to tell me whether that's true or not?"

All the indecision was gone from Victoria's face now. She glanced around the room, seeing the police actually for the first time, seeing what their presence meant. She looked Frank Vanness over slowly. He had played his trump card with her, let her know what he thought of her, and she was no longer awed by him, or afraid of him. All that was in the chilled glance she gave him. The sugary sweetness had disappeared, and I saw that Victoria was thinking fast.

Why didn't she answer him? What did she expect to gain by refusing to answer?

She smiled oddly, looked at me and then back at Vanness.

"I won't answer," she told him evenly.

"Victoria!" The word burst out of me. I could hear myself

yelling that name despairingly as I walked down the corridor toward the electric chair.

"It's all right," she said. "I'm sure, Charley, you will agree. I don't have to answer any questions until I have talked to my counsel."

Vanness laughed. "Brower your lawyer, Victoria?"

"Yes. He is. I want to talk to him before I answer any questions that will tend to degrade or incriminate me."

He laughed again. "There he is. Talk to him."

She shook her head. "Alone. I'm not going to talk to him in front of all these policemen."

Vanness seemed to be enjoying himself. He spoke to Bigley. "Let them talk in that room there. Keep the door ajar, and stand where you can watch them."

"I think you better start by telling me the truth," Victoria said.

"I've told you the truth."

"Charley, you're in a bad spot. A very bad spot. It was bad enough when I thought it was Cora who was dead down there in Florida."

"You know I didn't kill Laura Meadill. I was with you."

"Yes. But there are too many things I don't know. In the first place, you told me on the phone before you ever left here with Cora that you were going to get a divorce. But all the talk I've heard since then was that you and Cora were on a trial second honeymoon that didn't work out, and that she left you and went to Florida."

"You know how rumors get around."

"All right. I was willing to believe they were rumors, because I knew something that these people didn't know. I knew I held aces. I had something you wanted. I believed you had parted with Cora because I had what you couldn't get—not without me. You wanted to be a judge. I believed you were telling me the truth. Now I don't know."

"Why should I lie to you?"

"Suppose you tell me the truth and let's find out. Why not start by telling me why Laura Meadill was in Florida, posing as your wife, getting a divorce in her name?"

"I don't know."

"Charley, you're smarter than this. I always thought you

one of the smartest lawyers I know. Now you sound like a schoolboy caught in his first lie."

"I swear I don't know who killed Laura Meadill."

Her voice lowered. "Maybe we better clear up about Laura first."

I felt myself go cold all over. I waited, watching her.

"I suspected you from that first day you met me at the Brahma, Charley. I'd tried too long to get you, and you gave me the brush. Suddenly you were chasing me. There had to be a reason. I couldn't stand not knowing. So I found out you were dating your pretty little secretary. I had you followed, all those times when you were letting people believe you were with me."

"My God, Victoria—"

"You sound beat, Charley. You had me right where you wanted me. What woman could tell the truth—that she was *alone* in places like Atlantic City, waiting for you when you didn't show up? Oh, you had me pegged. I was too vain. I'd never tell anybody the truth about where you really were. I should have hated you, Charley, and I did. But I was intrigued. I knew this was leading to something. You were using me, and I hated you for that too. But I wanted to see what you expected to gain. Your little secretary running off to Florida—you following her—and all the time people were whispering that you were with me."

"Why did you let me get away with it?"

"Oh, Charley, you don't sound like yourself at all. I told you. I was waiting. I wanted to see what you'd do, what you'd have the gall to do to me. Then Gulick Williams died and I saw that no matter what your plans had been, I could change them. Oh, I had you pegged, too, Charley. Selfish, ambition-driven Charley Brower. You think I didn't know how you hated Cora because you couldn't get your hands on her fortune all at once? But you had many things I loved, Charley, and I thought I could buy you. I could make you a circuit judge. I could start you to where you wanted to fly."

I didn't say anything. I wiped the back of my hand across my mouth. My brain felt as if it had turned to mush.

"So when you came back this time, I was sold, Charley. Cora was getting a divorce, and you and I could be together, and I could get that appointment for you. But not

now. Divorce scandal I could have handled. But murder—
and not even your wife, but your mistress. One of your
mistresses. Your secretary, your secret love, down in Florida, pretending to be your wife. I don't know now, Charley. You want me to go in there and tell the police that you
were with me all the weekend. Should I compromise
myself for you further after all you've done to me?"

"My God, Victoria. You've got to tell them the truth."

"Do I? Didn't you use me when it was a lie? I let people
believe you were with me when you weren't at all. You
were in a hotel somewhere with Laura. You were in Florida
with Laura. Why should I tell them you were with me in
Barrington Springs and hurt my reputation that much
more? You saw what that detective thought of me—a com-
mon strumpet as far as he was concerned, because of what
people have said about you and me. Should I make it
worse—let it get in the papers that you were with me for
another romantic weekend in Barrington Springs when you
don't intend to marry me, and never did?"

"My God, Victoria. You've got to."

"No, Charley. You're wrong. I don't have to. I've let you
use me for the last time—I get nothing out of it but hurt."

I caught her arm.

"Let me go, Charley. You hurt me."

"I've held you a lot harder than this."

"But then I wanted you to." She twisted free.

"Victoria, it's still your word against mine. I told them I
was with you. I had to."

"Well, that's too bad, because my word is better than
yours—and I'll say you were not with me."

"But you're crazy!"

"Am I! Then thank yourself, Charley. I wasn't crazy until
you started using me for a wrestling bag."

"The people at Barrington Springs—"

She laughed in my face. "Who saw you, Charley? A few
moments on the station platform. A bellboy who won't
remember, because I'll tell him to forget. I registered as a single. I ordered all our meals. Whom did you talk to, Charley?
Who saw you there? Who really saw you well enough to
swear that it was you—and not someone else who resembled
you. After all, it could have been anybody. I like your type."

I stared around the room. Nothing looked substantial. I thought the floor might give way and let me sink forever downward; but that would have been too easy.

My voice shook. "What do you want, Victoria?"

"What do you mean, what do I want?"

"You'll tell the truth. It's just got a price—what is it?"

She smiled. "That's better. I was happy when I thought I'd have you, Charley. I thought the judgeship would buy you. Now I can't offer you that . . ." She traced her fingers along my face. I shivered. "All I can offer you now, Charley, is an alibi that might save your life."

"What do you want?"

"You. That's it. Like most women, I'm a fool about one man. No matter what you are, you're what I want. I'm willing to destroy my reputation and say that you were with me in Barrington Springs—in a single room—but in exchange, I want a wedding. Simple, Charley, with few flowers, a few friends, and a ring."

I stared at her. I tried to breathe, but the scent of her perfume overwhelmed me. I almost gagged.

"Make up your mind, Charley. You think I won't hit back at you for the shameful way you've used me, try it. Just crowd me; you'll see."

It was late in the afternoon before Vanness returned. A police cruiser sat outside all day, but nobody spoke to me. I suppose I could have walked out the back door and kept walking. I don't know; I didn't try it.

I prowled the house trying to guess what Victoria was going to do. She'd let me know. I could marry her—or go to the chair.

I felt nothing but fatigue. You can take just so much at a time. I walked into the room where I'd killed Cora. I stared at myself in the mirror. You stupid, ignorant son of a bitch. I laughed aloud. Oh, you were smart. Cora could get a Florida divorce, visit South America, and then later you'd get a letter notifying you of her death. You'd have to substantiate the fact of her death, but space was in your favor, and bribes. It could have been done.

Sure there were angles. If Cora divorced me she'd naturally have changed her will. How'd I expect to collect half a million if this were true and I couldn't substantiate her death? But I hadn't hoped to collect through a will. We had a joint bank account, many of her stocks and bonds were negotiable—I could get plenty before I ever sent myself news of her death. No matter what the banks thought about my cleaning out our joint accounts, there was nothing they could do.

I wiped my hand across my eyes. They ached so terribly, but I knew I couldn't close them. If I slept I dreamed. Cora's rigid body would crowd me against a wall so that I must stay cramped and miserable until I woke up, sure I had screamed.

That was what I had left of my big plans. Don't rush. Don't stampede. It will take a long time. Five hundred grand is a big prize, and it will take time to do it right. But I was not moving slowly. I was rushing along, and time had lost meaning.

I scrubbed my hands over my face.

"What's the matter?"

A sound burst out of my throat. I trembled all over and heeled around.

Vanness stood in the doorway, watching me. The worst part of it was I had no idea how long he had been standing there. Maybe he had been there all the time. Maybe he had been behind me watching all day long.

"You look beat, Counsellor."

I stared at him, waiting. I wasn't stepping into any trap. He wasn't even going to get the time of day from me. Here was a boy going to have to carry the ball all the way.

"I been working, Counsellor."

"Yeah."

"Been a busy day. Had a whole team of detectives working. Even being a lawyer as you are, I guess you got no idea how much you can accomplish in one day with a team of trained detectives working on one thing."

I waited. My lips were parched, but I didn't dampen them.

"For instance I'll tell you something you didn't know. We matched up that picture of the man the Florida police were seeking. His name is Lou Recsetti. Mean anything to you, Counsellor?" I shook my head.

"Ought to. Now that he's in the case, I've changed a lot of my ideas. You know who he is?"

"No."

"You ought to keep up with crime more. Lou is a hoodlum. Two-time loser, served time for robbery. Just got out on parole a few months ago."

"What does that mean to me?"

He smiled, a grim look boxed as it was between sagging nostrils and jutting jaw. "It ought to mean a lot. His wife worked for you."

"Wife?"

He shrugged. "Why not? A girl has to work when her husband gets caught on a robbery and has to serve time."

Robbery. It came back to me. Laura telling me about her friend whose husband was up for parole, but needed help. Oh, brother. Laura was the friend, and Lou Recsetti was the husband. Small-time hoodlum. Robbery.

"Only thing is that this Laura was afraid you might have heard of her husband. When she came here to Summit, she neglected to bring her married name with her. She took back her old name. Come to think of it, the old name wasn't much better."

When they start, they don't leave you anything.

"Laura wasn't exactly an angel, herself. She spent some time in the reformatory for girls."

I shook my head. He stared at me and nodded, pleased with himself. "You didn't know much about her at all, did you? That's where they taught her typing and shorthand. Rehabilitation stuff. She had quite a story. Seems she'd been her uncle's sweetie for a long time, since she was about fourteen."

I pressed my fist against my throat.

"It might never have come to light. But Uncle up and killed his wife, Laura Meadill's aunt. It happened a long time ago; no reason you should have heard about any of it. But seems at the trial Uncle broke down and admitted he had been making love to his wife's niece for a couple years.

They couldn't prove she had anything to do with the murder, or even knew anything about it. But the judge put her in the school for girls so that she could be given training and rehabilitation. What a laugh! While she was in the reformatory she met Lou Recsetti's sister, and when he came to visit, she met Lou. Pretty picture, eh, Counsellor?"

I shook my head, thinking of all the lies I had once believed about Laura, and all the truths I was forced to believe now.

"If I had known about Recsetti from the first, I could have been easier on you, Brower."

"What?"

"Sure. This punk being in this case changes everything. I got no more respect for you. I don't like you. I don't like men that can't live by moral laws—and you broke them with your wife. But I've changed my mind. I don't think you're guilty of murder. Recsetti gives me the hookup I need."

I stared at him, shaking my head.

He grinned, and I shivered at the humorless picture it made.

"Don't be dense, Brower. Like I say, I don't like you. But now I think you were being taken. I don't know all the angles yet, but I will."

"Taken?"

"Sure. This Laura Recsetti and her husband were setting you up like a pigeon in a barrel. I almost have to laugh—the smart lawyer getting set up like a pigeon. Maybe they planned it that way. Laura goes to work for you. Then they fix up some kind of deal to get your wife out of the way— and I got bad news for you on that. Down at the office they all agree on one thing. Your wife is dead."

"Why—why do they think so?"

"It stands to reason. They killed Mrs. Brower so they could let Laura pass as your wife down there in Florida. They were getting a divorce. Maybe the next step was to send a draft with Mrs. Brower's forged signature to the bank and withdraw as much of her money as they could—and get away to some country where they have no extradition." His laugh was hard. "Maybe they'd go to South America, and then send you word that your wife was there."

"But—you don't know my wife has been murdered."

"We know this. We know Laura Recsetti was posing as Mrs. Brower, getting a divorce. And take that letter the woman next door got. I've already found out that your wife never wrote that letter. But we got some things that your little secretary had written—and they swear that the doll that wrote the letter to Mrs. Myers also wrote all the specimens of handwriting we gathered from Laura Recsetti's apartment. That's good enough for me. It would have been good enough for the D.A. if she had lived."

"But if what you say is true why did Lou kill—his wife?"

"Still hurt to say it, Counsellor? I don't know yet. But the FBI is looking for Lou. When we get him, we'll find out what he was thinking. We'll pull that baby's thoughts out of him with a cold tweezers. Maybe they fought. Maybe Laura caught the clever-bug from working with you. Maybe she was trying to cross Lou. But the thing is, we got him in a plot to kill your wife—maybe even to kill you after you had collected your wife's money—what they left to you. We're looking for Lou. We'll find him."

"But—you still don't know that he killed her."

"Who else? He was living across the patio from her. Everybody down there was gossiping about the time they spent together. After she was killed—and before she was found—he disappeared."

"But you told me that I might have—"

"Ain't you got troubles enough, Brower, without taking on my worries? You told me that Victoria Haines would alibi you for the weekend.

"You haven't talked to her yet?"

"I told you. I been busy, digging into the pretty past of your secretary. I'll get around to her."

"Sure." I leaned against a wall.

"Right now, she ain't what's troubling me. What I'm worried about right now, whether you are or not, is your wife. What we want to know is what happened to her after you quarreled and you came back home alone."

"I don't know."

"Sure, and you haven't cared. You got the scent of this Victoria Haines. And all the time a hood and his woman are setting you up either for murder or extortion. All the time they have followed you—Lou must have—took over with Cora after you two fought and you came home. Somewhere he has killed her and hidden her body. That's got to be the answer. And now we're going to find out for sure and wrap this case up."

"But how, if you can't find her?"

"That's it. We're going to find her. We're going to send a description of her Buick on the wire to every police department in the country. When a crime happens far enough away from here sometimes we get only a whisper of it, nothing to go on. But we're going all out on this. We're having pictures made of Cora Brower—thousands of them. Somebody will remember her. And when that somebody comes forward, we can really slip the hooks to Recsetti. Not for one murder, but two."

I closed my eyes. I couldn't think of anything but Cora sprawled out on the front seat of that 1950 Studebaker, twelve hundred miles away in Kansas. They hadn't been able to trace her back to Summit, but now they would have her picture. The Kansas police and the FBI must have taken pictures of her when her body was found.

What if they caught Recsetti? What if they got him to admit killing Laura. He'd never admit killing Cora. But suppose Laura had told him all the things she and I had planned. Suppose he knew the truth, and to save himself, he talked to the police. Why, it would be easy to make them believe I had killed Laura.

That was what stopped me, because when Victoria Haines got through telling Vanness I had not been with her over the weekend, that would put another tint on the picture. Recsetti didn't even have to be smart. If he kept his mouth shut long enough, the stupidest cop on the force would come up with the answer: I had killed Laura in a fit of jealousy when I found out she was working with Recsetti.

I was tired. I had never been so tired in all my life. Not even the nightmare of driving twelve hundred miles without sleep, after a sleepless night, compared with the fatigue I felt at that moment.

I wanted to tell the truth. I was too tired to mess with it any more. All I had to do was say, "Vanness, I killed Cora." That was all I had to do. It would be over then and I could rest.

But I couldn't. Vanness stood staring at me, but I was too tired to open my mouth.

When I looked up again, Vanness was gone. I did not even know for how long. I ran through the bedroom door. For a minute I completely lost my head. I wanted to yell for Vanness. I didn't want him to go out of this house and leave me here. What was the sense in waiting? It was just a matter of time, wasn't it?

"Frank?"

There was no answer. The sound of my voice struck the walls and battered to nothingness. I ran out on the veranda. The police cruiser was gone, too.

But I didn't feel any better. They had me. I could stay in this house, sleepless, waiting. Or I could yell until they came back for me. Everything I had wanted was gone, everything I had tried to win was lost.

I looked around the house. I was alone. Perhaps for the very last time in whatever time was left to me I was alone. If I was going to do anything, this was the moment.

What could I do? Was there any sense in running? I was never going to be a judge in anybody's court. I was never going to have that half-million dollars Cora had been hoarding. Laura was dead. I was no longer Charles R. Brower, attorney. I was Charley Brower, wanted for murder.

But at least I was still alive.

I looked at my watch. I could probably catch a plane north to Canada, west to the Coast, or south to Miami. South? Why not south? Who'd think I was going to run in the direction they already wanted me? Who'd look for me down there?

My mouth twisted. Don't try to outsmart anybody, Brower. You tried that, the big smart lawyer, taking care of all the angles. Look where it got you.

Run. But don't try to be smart about it. Just be fast. If you hurry, you might make it.

How much time did I have? There was no way to know that. Maybe when Vanness talked to Victoria and she denied being with me he would come back and pick me up. Maybe they wouldn't arrest me until after they had caught Recsetti. In that case I had a few hours, a few days. It wasn't much, but if I hurried it might be enough.

I looked around. It was dark now; the darkness smoked through the house. If I ran, it would be an admission of guilt. But why split hairs? Admit it or have it proved? If you were in Pakistan, it didn't matter what they proved.

They might come looking for me. But it would take time, and time was all I wanted. Time to rest. Only now I couldn't rest. I had to get out of here.

I grabbed a checkbook, and let the door slam behind me.

I threw open the garage door and got into my car. My hands shook so badly I dropped the ignition keys, had to fumble on the floor for them.

I started the car, switched on the lights. Something warned me they might be watching and it was dark enough to get to the street without being seen if I cut the lights. Then I remembered the back-up lights would burn if I put the car in reverse. But it was a chance I had to take.

I reversed the car, moving slowly down the drive and out into the street.

I changed gears, moved along Forest Drive. A car moved out in front of me from Sixty-fifth. It pulled out and did not slow down though it was marked. At first I thought it was cops. I stared at the car. It was big, and a dark shade. Not official.

I slammed on brakes, pulled around and tried to go in front of it.

That was when I saw the car come the other way from Sixty-fifth. It pulled up so I had to stop. The two black cars made a wedge and I was caught.

Before I could reverse, two men were standing at the side of my car. My stomach turned over.

"Just let it sit," one of them said.

"You guys are blocking—"

"Just let it sit. Turn off that engine."

I stared at them. Their eyes were dead in expressionless faces. I cut the motor. The silence pressed in.

"What do you want?"

"What's your name?" One of them said.

"You guys can't do anything like this. There are people along this street."

"You heard me, fellow. I asked you a question. What's your name?"

The other opened the door. I caught at it, but he wrenched it free, stepped inside, and leaned against it.

"Your name Richard Smith?"

I knew then. They didn't have to extend engraved business cards. I saw there were four others in the two black cars. All of them from the hot-car ring, from the man whose name I'd forced out of Mike Welch.

You ever buy a car under that name? Nineteen-fifty Studebaker? Pay cash for it by telegram?"

"I don't know what you're talking about."

He grabbed my shirt suddenly and dragged me from the car. I stumbled and hit the pavement on my knees. I tried to get up, but he twisted his fist, pressing down.

Look, Mr. Smith. Right in that car over there."

They had left the rear door of one of the cars opened. I saw Mike Welch sitting in the back seat. He looked battered. He stared at me, and his eyes were cold.

I made a noise in my throat.

"Listen, Mr. Smith. The boss sent us to talk to you. Seems you got him in a bad mess. Had the Feds breathing all over him. He don't like that. Bad for business."

The back of his hand across my face would have knocked me over, but he would not release me.

"Yeah. Real bad for business. Boss said we was to impress on you. He don't like nothing that hurts his business."

They dragged me up and fists worked me over, stomach and back.

"Boss pays a lot of money for protection. He likes things smooth. He don't like it when somebody makes him trouble."

It was as if my insides were being seared. The hood released me and I crumpled, my knees hitting the pavement.

"Get up, Mr. Smith."

He reached down, caught my tie and twisted it until I couldn't breathe. Slowly I got to my feet.

"That's better."

The fists started again. The tie was twisted and the fists worked swiftly, professionally.

I flailed out with my arms, no longer able to breathe.

"Stand still, Mr. Smith."

Those hands went back and forth across my face. The tie twisted tighter. When they started using their knees the agony was too terrible. I no longer felt it.

They released me and I hit the ground hard, flopping around as I tried to get my breathing started again.

Everytime I moved, one of them kicked me, in the head or in the stomach. It didn't seem to matter to them. I couldn't lie still because I could not breathe again unless I moved. But finally I realized they were going to keep beating and kicking me as long as I moved.

I lay still, gasping for breath. They kicked me again. But they seemed to have gone far away. My head spun, my arm twitched, and again they kicked me. Then I was like slime on the street, without bones or muscles.

They lifted me, shoved me back under the steering wheel of my car. They started the engine and put it in gear. The car rolled slowly forward, going crazily down Forest Drive until it bumped the curb, rolled up on the parkway and came to a stop against a tree.

Finally I could breathe again. I sat up but the agony flashed through me and I almost passed out. I tried to start the car, tried to drive, but I couldn't. I managed to open the door. I let myself fall to the parkway. At last I tried to stand, but when I did the night wheeled around me and I knew I couldn't walk.

I took a step and fell flat on my face.

I stared back through the dark street to my driveway. It seemed an impossible distance. I crawled over into the darkness and moved on my hands and knees all the way to my yard.

I got up then, staggered and fell, got up, staggered and fell, until I was back in the house.

Inside the door, I fell and lay there until I could breathe again. It hurt, but I could do it.

At last I pulled myself up and started, dragging myself along the wall to my bedroom.

Suddenly a light from the front room struck me in the face.

I was too tired to care, too tired even to react.

"Well, lover boy. Look at lover boy. Lover boy, you look bad. You look like you just caught your death of knuckles."

I opened my eyes and stared at him. He was standing inside the front room door. Beyond him I saw the blinds were tightly drawn. He looked haggard, but he was in better shape than I was. His clothes looked mussed and sweated. His collar was still turned up about his neck. But I recognized Lou Recsetti. He was a man on the run. He looked it.

"What are you doing here?" Blood ran out of my mouth when I spoke.

"Came to see you, lover."

I laughed at him, and punched at my aching teeth with my fingers.

"What you got to laugh at, lover?"

"You. You had any sense you'd be out of this country. Cops are looking for you."

"Let 'em look. Exercise won't hurt 'em. Most cops look like slobs because they don't get enough exercise. So let 'em look. Just don't waste my time. I ain't got a lot of it."

"They know you killed Laura."

"Do they? You think it's going to do them much good?" He laughed. "You think it's going to do you much good?"

I didn't answer him. I leaned against the wall, just feeling good because I could breathe again.

"Look, lover boy. You don't look like you can take very much more. And I'm a boy knows tricks that'll hurt you in new places. I got no temper; all I want from you is money. As much of Cora Brower's money as you can get your hands on."

"Right now?" I laughed at him. "None of it."

"Okay. So tomorrow you get it. I'm out of the country—you don't see me any more."

"What makes you think I can get Cora's money?"

"What makes you think I'm going to argue with you about it? Cora won't care. I know that. Out there in Kansas, she's past caring."

I stared at him. Laura had told him everything. He read my thoughts.

"That's right, she didn't hold back on her Lou. No more than you will when you know the things I can do to your nerves. She even told me you have a joint bank account with Cora."

"All I'd have to do is draw a big amount with Cora missing and I'd have the cops all over me."

"Oh, stop dreaming, lover. It's just a matter of time until you've got them on you anyhow. So look at it the smart way. Money ain't going to do you any good, but it'll help me get out of the country. Ordinarily, I'd be greedy. I'd take it all. But my little trouble with Laura changes that, and I'll settle for enough to get me beyond the reach of these cops. Now stop stalling. You want trouble, just stall. That's what our girl Laura did. Tried to stall me."

He tried to laugh, but his face worked with something that was not laughter. His voice remained taut.

"I wanted her to come back up here and put the big squeeze on you and we'd clear out. But she wouldn't do it. Want to hear something funny, lover? She fell for you. Man, the way she fell for you!"

It was self-torture, but he couldn't stop.

"Man, you should have seen that little scene when she told me she wouldn't put the arm on you for all that loot." He shook his head. "She changed after she went to work for you. Got too classy for Lou—tried to deal me out. But I'd never have killed her—not until she pushed me too hard."

I stared at him for a long time. I said slowly, "I'm no good, Recsetti. Maybe I never knew how rotten I was until you walked in here. I can look at you and see what I am. I don't like it. I fooled myself with a lot of fine talk but all the time I was slimy, like you. But this is it. You killed

Laura. That's too bad, because I'm going to fix you, for Laura."

He stood there, watching me. I managed to straighten up. I walked the seven long paces to the telephone. I was sweating.

"Run, Lou," I said. "I'm calling the cops. I'm too beat to run, too tired to fight any more. You're right. I'm not going to get away. But you aren't either."

He sprang through the doorway and lunged at me. His fist knocked the receiver from my hand. He slapped the telephone off the table.

I grabbed at him. His right hand was in his pocket. I caught at it. It covered a gun.

I tried to hold it pushed against the bottom of his pocket. But I didn't have strength enough. His left fist caught me beside the head and spun me around.

I closed my fingers on that gun hand, holding on. I stumbled around, falling away from him and clinging to that gun. I heard a sound like a muffled shot.

The impact in the small of my back sent me sprawling forward. It tore my grasp loose from Recsetti's pocket and knocked me off my feet.

I carried the small table with me. I struck against the wall and slid down it slowly.

I struck on my knees and tried to turn, but couldn't. The movement made me dizzy and I toppled on my side. Gradually I saw the fuzzy outline of Recsetti standing staring down at me. He said something, but I didn't hear what it was. There was this terrible pounding in my ears. I kept telling myself I had to get up, but I couldn't force my legs to move. Distantly I heard the front door slam.

I lay there cursing myself. Never able to do anything you vow. You were going to get away with murder and collect half a million dollars, and you couldn't do that. You were going to stop Recsetti because he killed Laura.

I tried to force myself to my feet, but no message reached my legs at all. I could lie there feeling the tears well up in my eyes and spill down my cheeks.

Abruptly there were sounds like thunder from my front yard. But they were not thunder, they were too rapid, too sharply defined, too near for thunder.

It was gunfire.

I tried to smile. Recsetti had run into trouble, that was sure.

I lay writhing. Die? Me? I can tell you this. People die only when they don't want to die.

I saw the front door open. I had a strange view of it from the floor. I saw their feet first, and their legs. Then I saw it was police and they carried Recsetti's bullet riddled body.

Frank Vanness said something to them and they dropped Recsetti's body as if he were something they'd killed in the woods.

Vanness came along the hall. I watched his legs move, his feet. He bent down beside me.

"Brower's been shot," he said. "In the spine, looks like. Better call a doctor."

Sure, I thought, keep me alive. Pamper me. All the way to the electric chair.

A couple of days later, Dr. Ed Murray gave me the diagnosis.

"The bullet splintered your spine, near the base," Ed said. "At that, you were lucky."

"Sure"

"You're alive. You can't walk, you'll be confined to a wheelchair or bed the rest of your life. But there are compensations. You're good for some things. Reading. Talking. It's just that you're never going to walk any more."

Frank Vanness was beaming. He sat in the white hospital chair beside my bed.

"Like I told you, Brower. We cleaned it up. All the way up. We got a report Recsetti was headed this way. It didn't make sense but we put a stake-out. I figured he was trying to take you for something and came here to do it."

I didn't say anything. In the days since Recsetti shot me, I had done some heavy thinking about him, and about Laura and me. Laura had whatever it is that drives the men who love her off their rocker. I know what she did to me. Maybe that's what she did to Lou. It must have driven him crazy when he learned his wife had fallen in love with me and was walking out on him. And then he had come up here to Summit.

I thought about it, and it seemed to be that he had done to me just what he wanted to do. If he could have gotten money from me, he would have taken it, sure. But what was the most he could hope for, knowing the setup with Cora's money? A few thousand bucks at the most. Not very much, compared to his life. But he hadn't been thinking about his life. He wanted to hit at the guy who'd taken Laura from him.

He had forgotten about escape. He had killed Laura in that raging jealousy, but that hadn't been enough. I was still alive, and he could not rest until he had evened that score.

It looked about even. . . .

Vanness said, "What do you think about it?"

"About what?"

"Haven't you been listening to me?"

"Should I have been?"

"Listen, Brower, I knew you lawyers think us cops are stupid. But I got news for you. If it hadn't been for all the work I done on this case you'd be headed for the electric chair right now."

I stared at him, speechlessly.

"That's right," he said, misunderstanding my look. "Now, Recsetti got killed trying to get away from your house, so he can't confess. But we have to build his story the way it has to be. But there are a lot of crazy angles, and some people were hot to elect you as the killer."

"But not you?"

"Not me. I figure you're stupid enough to chase skirts, but not stupid enough to murder. But here's the catch. With Lou as the killer, there are too many unexplained angles. But I finally convinced them that he had planned some kind of extortion after he killed your wife—"

"Killed my wife?"

"Yeah, we cleared that one. Mrs. Brower was killed and

left out in a Kansas wheatfield. Now that's just the kind of
thing Recsetti would pull. I'll say this for him; part of it was
clever. An Indiana license plate, stolen from a car in Florida.
That checks, he was down there. A stolen car, gotten from
his hood friends. He had an in with them. The kind of in
only another hood would have. There was no way to tie
that car down. I mean *no* way. The FBI tried all its tests,
road dirt, film, fingerprints, and nothing checked out. Your
wife and that car seemed to belong nowhere. They even got
desperate enough to test the water in the radiator."

"What for?"

"Mineral deposits. They found out that car used no
water, and that meant it didn't boil and was kept cool. So
the chemists figured maybe the chemicals had not deposited out. They tell me water in Florida is unlike water in
North Carolina, and water in New York has a lot of minerals
not found in Chicago water. Anyway they hoped to get
within a region. Then they were going to send pictures of
Cora to all those regions. Maybe they'd hit. They had failed
every other way.

"But the minerals had deposited out. At least some of
them had. The chemists tried, but they couldn't be sure.
But then they found something."

I just looked at him, did not speak.

"The stuff that somebody had put in the radiator to be
sure it didn't leak—you know what? It's manufactured in
this area. The Federal Trade Commission hasn't permitted
the manufacturer to ship it yet, so to exist, he's been selling
it to hot-car rings so they can doctor up old wrecks. So, just
when we were planning to send out Cora's picture it came
to us."

"And you know Lou Recsetti did it?"

"It adds. Nothing else adds. Not to me. No matter what
they said about you. I figured you were chasing the Haines
babe. You did a lot of screwy things—but none of them
added up to murder. Not quite."

"Did Victoria say I was with her that weekend?"

"Well, now, that was a funny thing. First when I went to
talk with her, she said you were not with her. I can tell you
it looked bad."

"But she changed her mind?"

His jaw jutted. "I told you I'd get the truth, didn't I? I know how to handle women. First I found out what proved to me you didn't kill either your wife or the Recsetti woman. Then I went back and camped with Haines. She changed her story. Seems that she didn't want to compromise her reputation—her words. She didn't want it spread in the papers that she had been at Barrington Springs with you. But I told her she was sending you to the chair unless she told the truth. I explained to her why I knew you hadn't killed your wife—and then she broke down and told me you were with her from Saturday to Monday morning."

I should have felt better. I didn't. I didn't ask him what his final proof was that I was innocent. I was ripped up wanting to know, but I knew better than to ask.

Vanness nodded. "You could have saved yourself some trouble if you'd spoken up. I had to hear it from your neighbor."

"Edie?"

"That's right. Mrs Myers. That was one of the reasons she was so sure that Cora had not gone off to Florida. She told Mrs. Myers the last evening Mrs. Myers saw her that she was going to fix her will before she left and Mrs. Myers said she never did it, never got to. You must have known, but you didn't tell us your wife had changed her will when you started running around with Victoria Haines."

I closed my eyes. Sure. That was Cora. Afraid something might happen to her and I would get that half-million dollars. It was right in character. I could hear her telling Edie Myers that Haines woman would never get her hands on that money.

Vanness said, "You knew your wife had left her money to charity. So I knew you had not done it. You just didn't have a motive."

Victoria came that night at eight. She brought flowers. Combined with her perfume, the odor became intolerable.

"I hope we don't have to wait too long, darling," Victoria said in a voice like a dull knife edge.

"Wait? For what?"

"To be married, darling. I might get impatient."

I tried to laugh. "Would you change your story again?"

She shrugged "I might add to it. After all, I know so much more. I know that you said Cora was leaving you—on the same night she was telling everybody you were going on a second honeymoon. If I told all that, darling, it would all start again, only I don't think it would end quite the same."

"Why do you want me?" In my mind I was wailing in despair. "You know all about me. You know what I am. You must know that Cora's money will go to charity and there's no way I can stop it. Look at what's left of me."

She smiled, leaning forward. My nostrils distended. "Oh, you're not so bad. I talked to Dr. Murray, darling. Before I changed my story for Vanness, I found out that you're fine. You'll be in bed, but I couldn't ask for anything more. That's where I like you best. I'll always know where you are. You won't be out catting around. And as for money—we don't need Cora's, darling. I don't have her fortune, but the settlement you got me from Chet will keep us quite adequately. After all, darling, we don't need much. We'll have each other."

I tried to tell myself I'd get used to it.

But a week after Victoria and I were married, I felt the way I had the night the hoods beat the breath out of me. I couldn't live without some fresh air. There was nothing but the cloying perfume, no matter what I did in Victoria's house. It was everywhere.

I wheeled myself into the bathroom. The scent was more potent in here, but I was not going to be long. I pulled myself up, got a package of razor blades. I was hacking at my wrists when Victoria ran in and knocked them from my hands. I lay my head back, gasping for fresh air.

"It's all right, darling" She wheeled me back into that frilly bedroom, the curtains, the pictures, everything feminine and dainty and scented. "I know you feel lost, and cheated. You think your life is over just because you can't get around and walk. You don't need to. We're together, darling. For always. I'll be near you, taking care of you. Come, darling, let me love you—you'll be so glad you're alive."

That day she bought an electric razor. Since then she's

watched me closely. She pretends she isn't, but she never lets me out of her sight, never lets me get far enough away so I can get a deep breath of fresh air.

All I live for now is the moment when she'll get careless. She'll forget to watch me, and I'll find some way to kill myself. There's got to be a way. I can't breathe any more in this bedroom, and she won't let me out of it alone.

I think about Lou Recsetti, and I know he was lucky. He paid for his crimes fast. He got it over with. But me? I'm paying bit by bit. I'm probably the only guy who ever longed for the electric chair. Every day I wake up and I pay a little more, only I go on paying, and it never ends, never ceases for a moment.

She comes upon me and slips her arms about me, and she never gets tired. There's no way to escape her. She keeps at me, and nothing discourages her. She invents a hundred new ways to excite me, as she calls it.

One thing. I can sleep. I can't breathe but I can sleep. Sometimes I dream about Cora, but it's not so bad. I no longer wake up screaming when I dream about Cora.

No. Not me. I don't wake up screaming.

With me, it's a little different. Deep inside my mind where Victoria can't hear me, I scream myself to sleep.

THE END

VINTAGE CRIME / **BLACK LIZARD**

VINTAGE CRIME / **BLACK LIZARD**

___ **The Talented Mr. Ripley** $10.00   0-679-74229-8
     by Patricia Highsmith

___ **A Rage in Harlem** by Chester Himes $8.00   0-679-72040-5

___ **Shattered** by Richard Neely $9.00   0-679-73498-8

___ **The Laughing Policeman** $9.00   0-679-74223-9
     by Maj Sjöwall and Per Wahlöö

___ **The Locked Room** $10.00   0-679-74222-0
     by Maj Sjöwall and Per Wahlöö

___ **After Dark, My Sweet** $7.95   0-679-73247-0
     by Jim Thompson

___ **The Alcoholics** by Jim Thompson $8.00   0-679-73313-2

___ **The Criminal** by Jim Thompson $8.00   0-679-73314-0

___ **Cropper's Cabin** by Jim Thompson $8.00   0-679-73315-9

___ **The Getaway** by Jim Thompson $8.95   0-679-73250-0

___ **The Grifters** by Jim Thompson $8.95   0-679-73248-9

___ **A Hell of a Woman** by Jim Thompson $10.00   0-679-73251-9

___ **The Killer Inside Me** $9.00   0-679-73397-3
     by Jim Thompson

___ **Nothing More Than Murder** $9.00   0-679-73309-4
     by Jim Thompson

___ **Pop. 1280** by Jim Thompson $9.00   0-679-73249-7

___ **Recoil** by Jim Thompson $8.00   0-679-73308-6

___ **Savage Night** by Jim Thompson $8.00   0-679-73310-8

___ **A Swell-Looking Babe** $8.00   0-679-73311-6
     by Jim Thompson

___ **Wild Town** by Jim Thompson $9.00   0-679-73312-4

___ **The Burnt Orange Heresy** $7.95   0-679-73252-7
     by Charles Willeford

___ **Cockfighter** by Charles Willeford $9.00   0-679-73471-6

___ **Pick-Up** by Charles Willeford $7.95   0-679-73253-5

___ **The Hot Spot** by Charles Williams $8.95   0-679-73329-9